FIVE SUTRAS OF JESUS:

DISCOVERING THE CHRIST THE CHURCH FORGOT

ROBERT MICHAEL MAYOR

Dearest Jewn,
thank you for being
a living encounter of the
Divine. Blessings on the
way!

Published by Angel's Share Publishing.

All quotations of scripture are from the New Revised Standard Version Bible: Anglicized Edition, copyright 1989, 1995, Division of Christian Education of the National Council of the Churches of Christ in the United States of America. Used by permission. All rights reserved.

Cover Photo Copyright © Dudarev Mikhail/Shutterstock.com. Used by permission.

Library of Congress Control Number: 2013906978

ISBN 978-0-615-80303-6

First edition.

DEDICATION

For Liana and Justin
in whom I meet the Divine on a daily basis

ACKNOWLEDGEMENTS

No book is strictly the work of any one person. It always occurs within the context of a community. This work is no exception and I would be remiss if I didn't acknowledge the people without whom this book would never have occurred.

To start, many, many thanks go to the good people of All Saints Episcopal Church in Salt Lake City who had the courage and wisdom to encourage me to write this book, provided the sabbatical necessary for its initial penning, and gave feedback on the book in its initial form.

Next, a word of thanks to my good friend the Rev. Michael Jackson who saw in me the potential for the work I did and the necessity for the sabbatical which allowed it. Thank you for being a kindred spirit and for never letting me forget my deepest vocation.

Also, much thanks to my good friends from the UK, Michael and Carole Blackwell who supported my work in myriad ways. Your enthusiasm, friendship, and willingness to read and edit were of immense help.

Next, a great deal of thanks to the good people of Westcott House Theological College in Cambridge, England for providing a library, resources, and eager and willing ears to support the work of writing the book.

Thank you to the several dozen readers of the various drafts of this book for your patience, honesty, and willingness to challenge my writing and me.

Finally, thank you to my dear wife Liana and my son Justin for whom I have dedicated this book. Your sacrifice was great for this project. Thank you for your love and support, you were my muses and are the support of my very soul.

TABLE OF CONTENTS

Dedication iii
Acknowledgements..v
Chapter 1: Reflections of a Preacher..1

PART I: FIVE CORE TEACHINGS **9**
Chapter 2: Reading With a Second Naïveté 11
Chapter 3: The Shape of a Life Lived 25
Chapter 4: Teaching, Sutra, and Köan 31
Chapter 5: A Summary of the Five Sutras of Jesus.....................................43

PART II: ALL THERE IS IS NOW **47**
Chapter 6: The Burden of Being Self-Conscious – Living With Mortality..........49
Chapter 7: The Past is a Memory and the Future is a Fantasy 59
Chapter 8: Today - The Gift of Eternity 65

PART III: YOU ARE ADORED BY THE DIVINE AND THERE IS NOTHING YOU CAN DO TO CHANGE IT **73**
Chapter 9: Separation From God as an Explanation of Death 75
Chapter 10: God as Father..81
Chapter 11: Love One Another as I Have Loved You.................................87

PART IV: YOUR RELATIONSHIP WITH GOD IS ABOUT YOUR RELATIONSHIP WITH OTHERS **93**
Chapter 12: The Parable Tradition...95
Chapter 13: The Summary of the Law...103
Chapter 14: Who is my Neighbor? 109

PART V: MORALITY IS ABOUT RELATIONSHIPS, NOT RULES **119**
Chapter 15: Why Have Rules?..121
Chapter 16: Breaking the Rules for the Sake of Relationships 129
Chapter 17: The Sabbath was Created for Humans, Not Humans for the
Sabbath 137

PART VI: THE KINGDOM OF GOD IS AT HAND....................................**145**
Chapter 18: What is the Kingdom of God? 147
Chapter 19: "At Hand" and "Within" - Metaphors for Human Agency...........159
Chapter 20: Always and Never..165

TABLE OF CONTENTS (CONT.)

PART VII: A POST-NICENE CHRISTIANITY **171**
Chapter 21: Was Jesus a Teacher of Sutras?..173
Chapter 22: Origins of the Western Jesus and an Alternative 179
Chapter 23: Moving From Belief in Ideas to a Relationship With a Deeper
Reality 187
Bibliography 195
Notes..197

CHAPTER 1:
REFLECTIONS OF A PREACHER

Who is Jesus of Nazareth? A first-century rabbi? A religious zealot? A wisdom teacher? The savior of the world? The son of God? A Jewish bodhisattva? On some level he is all of these things, and equally he is none of them. Each of those words represents a label, which not only brings meaning, but also limits it. Contrary to what the most strident voices of Christianity and secularism would have us believe, the truth of Jesus of Nazareth is a mystery. Jesus is, at this point in the human story, something like a large movie screen upon which we project anything and everything.

There's no shortage of books about Jesus. It doesn't matter what you want to read (liberal theology, conservative theology, academic studies of scripture, the historical Jesus, politics, spirituality, etc.) there is likely a book to be found on the topic. Each of these books offers some "truth" about Jesus. Many claim to have the definitive answer. In the crashing noise of all those voices it can be hard to have any experience that might genuinely be described as spiritual. And so you can imagine why it has taken several years of encouragement and cajoling by others to write the book you now hold in your hands.

What you will find in the chapters that follow will not prove some deep historical reality about Jesus. Nor will it prove anything about the form or origin of the texts of the Bible either. It's not even an attempt to get at the "historical Jesus." Put simply, this is not an academic book. Instead, it is the reflection of one person who, for more than a decade and a half, has struggled to explore authentically the stories of Jesus found in the Bible, which I believe to be nothing more (nothing less either) than texts that have been inherited from past generations. It is informed by my experience as a priest in the Episcopal Church. It is informed by the breadth of my reading (secular, spiritual, scientific, and theological). It is informed by my personal experiences as a human being. And, in it is much of the content of my preaching over the last half-decade or more. Put simply, it is an exploration of what I have come to experience as the "good news" of the person of Jesus, his life and his message.

When I was awarded my professional graduate degree from seminary more than 15 years ago I could never have imagined the content that is contained in the pages that follow. Although, even then, I already had more than a general familiarity with the Bible, my images of Jesus and the Gospels were still heavily shaped by Western Christian tradition—a rich centuries-long tradition which has as much, if not more, to do with the history and cultures of Western Europe as with the witness of scripture.

And so, with all the arrogance that comes with youth empowered by education, I entered ordained ministry in the Episcopal Church convinced I knew and understood the core message of Jesus and the meaning of his life and death. It didn't take long for "the wheels to come off" that proverbial cart however. On a daily basis, theory gave way to reality. Caring for people spiritually and emotionally, and the practice of making sense of God in the world were no longer brain candy to be savored in the rarefied atmosphere of an academic institution. Instead, I was engaging real people living their real lives. These were people who were looking to me as a counselor, a spiritual mentor, and a teacher to help them make sense of their lives in relation to the Divine.

What I quickly discovered was that the comfortable images of God, and more specifically Jesus, with which I had grown up often left an image of the Divine that was negligent, abusive, and careless; or worse, a God that was irrelevant and unbelievable to anyone who took seriously the intellectual and scientific developments of the last century. Whether it was an 80-year-old woman with cancer asking why God was punishing her after so many years of faithful belief, or a 22-year-old grad student asking how to reconcile his sense of spirituality with the unbelievable supernaturalism of traditional religion, I realized that if there was any truth to the practice of Christian faith the old paradigms weren't going to work anymore.

As you might imagine, such an awakening left me struggling to find a place in which to be grounded. I had only recently committed my life to being a representative of belief in God, and moreover belief in Jesus as God, and already things were on the rocks. How could I remain in my position with such questions floating through my mind on almost a daily basis? And while I still had a sense of the reality of the Divine and something of the reality of Jesus' core nature as Divine, I also found myself searching for authentic and meaningful language that could communicate the deeper truths that arose from my real experiences and informed my faith. I wish I could say that I came at this dilemma with a plan. But, like I surmise most people do, I stumbled through for many years with my vision not much above the immediate demands of each day.

Throughout this time my own struggles with meaning not only continued, but only got more pronounced. Thanks to the work associated with being an ordained person, I was now regularly encountering disease and death in the lives of others. I was more than aware of the numerous biblical images of God miraculously intervening in human events. I was equally aware of the variety of traditions that argued for God's intervention for the faithful. But, as much as I wanted to believe in supernatural intervention, I never saw it. That is not to say that there weren't some really profound moments in the middle of those experiences, but genuinely supernatural events like those found in the scriptures never happened. At the same time, however, there was a growing sense of mystery around what I was experiencing. Whether it was the profound presence of life at the moment of death, the overwhelming sense of life (and sometimes joy) in a person facing a terminal illness, the deep wisdom of a child, the universe of meaning contained in a single encounter with another person, or any number of other paradoxical and mysterious experiences, I knew that there was more going on than wishful thinking, mental projection, quantum physics, or my own sense of mythology.

And so, while I was no longer completely satisfied with the tradition I was now called to represent, I found myself in the unenviable position of being able to find no better substitute. And even while I was deeply unhappy with the stale and disconnected realities of institutional religion, I continued to find this mysterious person of Jesus compelling. In the Gospels, perhaps only because they were comfortable and familiar, I heard the echoes of the Divine. Week after week in preparation for Sunday worship (and, more often than not, having to prepare a sermon) I was immersed in the stories about and the teachings of Jesus. In fact, thanks to being in a liturgical church with a three-year lectionary (a schedule of readings for Sunday services), I was exposed to the vast majority of the Bible again and again.

In the process of reading, reflecting, teaching, and engaging real people in their real lives something began to form. It literally took years to happen and was so subtle a process that I was caught completely unaware when the fullness of it began to surface. Starting in about my ninth year of ordained ministry, I began to get significant feedback about my preaching. Not the usual "nice sermon" comments or comments about style, but substantial remarks about the content. The overwhelming bulk of it was positive, but there was a noticeable increase in the negative as well. Those who appreciated what they were hearing seemed to be making the kind of connections that I had so wanted to try to assist. Those who were less appreciative often felt challenged by the scriptural images of Jesus that did not match up to the images that they held dear. What all the feedback had in common however was that it was specific, passionate, and connected to day-to-day living.

To be frank, I was initially puzzled by the increased response. My thinking at the time ran something along the lines of "all I'm doing is being as authentic as I can be with the text as I read it." In dialoguing with a small group of trusted colleagues and friends, however, I began to get feedback that indicated something much more was going on.

What I have come to recognize is that the Gospels are not the end of the journey towards Jesus but are, in fact, a jumping off point leading deeper "down the rabbit hole." In all the countless purposes they serve, the Gospels provide a starting place in the journey of faith. It is a place that we return to repeatedly as we move ever deeper into the mystery of who and what God is.

I used to think that the Gospels were static stories that conveyed a series of historical events. But I have come to realize that they are so much more than that and that there is nothing static about them. The Gospels are living texts, which invite the reader to enter the story and participate in it in the same way that a good novel invites the reader to come into the story and participate. The difference is that the Gospels exist not simply to entertain but to give us an opportunity to experience the Divine. And just as a great novel can be read at age 18 and have one meaning and then read again at age 25 and have another, or at age 40 and have yet another meaning, so too can the Gospels be read at different times in our lives and have new and surprising meaning. With each reading we will experience familiar things from our last visit and at the same time find whole new things as well. In each reading of the Gospels we may well experience a new dimension of the Divine we never expected.

The amazing thing is that when we approach the Bible from this perspective, questions of right or wrong belief (orthodoxy or heresy) no longer make sense, because we recognize the inherently vibrant nature of these very human texts and the deep mystery we encounter through them.

It is also abundantly clear to me at this point—as a large number of scholars would agree—that Jesus had no interest in the creation of a new religion with himself as the object of its worship. The decision to recognize Jesus as God, and to then place on him any number of theological and spiritual definitions, comes from those who followed and not from Jesus. To be clear, my point in bringing this up is not to wrestle with the question of the divinity of Jesus, but to raise the point that the idea that he is God does not come from him, but from others. And to the degree that we focus on his divinity exclusively, we risk skewing or outright missing important content from and about Jesus that is reported in the Gospels.

What does appear to be the case in regard to the life and message of Jesus, to the degree we can trust the texts of the Bible, is that he was concerned about how human beings lived. He was concerned about how human living is related to the Divine. He was concerned about all of the issues of social and human justice that arise when human beings choose to live mindfully in relation to one another and the Divine. Also, it seems clear, that he not only held to certain beliefs in regards to these ultimate concerns, but that he lived a life that was overtly and obviously in synch with what he taught.

This pattern, found in all four Gospels, has shaped my understanding as outlined above, as well as shaping the details that will follow. In fact, after reflecting on the Gospels many times, it has become clear to me that throughout them there are five core ideas which surface again and again, and it is virtually impossible to find in Jesus' teaching where at least one of these tenets is not either explicitly or implicitly found.

In order to explore fully and clearly how this can be the case we must first do some preliminary work in the first section of this book. It is my hope, in a cursory way, to invite you into the process I have gone through that led to the insights that will follow. First, we must abandon some preconceptions and prejudices that are common in the early part of the 21st century. To the degree that we are able, we must be willing to not only embrace the rational and observational methods of scripture study and the sciences, but we also must be willing to adopt what the 20th-century philosopher, Paul Ricoeur, refers to as a "second naïveté" in relation to a biblical text. By doing so we are able to use our imagination with the Gospel stories while not abandoning everything that rational thought and inquiry provide.

Because of the increasing popularity of Eastern religious thought in the West and its regular misapplication, we need to take time to explore the ways in which Jesus was an Eastern thinker and how his form of Eastern thought is like, as well as not like, other Eastern spiritual teaching. In examining this we can also explore the relationship of the Western concept of teaching and the Eastern ideas of sutra and kōan.

Having done that work we can outline the five core teachings (sutras) of Jesus and explore how each of them forms a thread upon which all the specific teachings and sayings of Jesus are held together.

The remainder of the book is divided into sections with every section containing three to four chapters. Each of these sections is dedicated to one of the sutras, with the chapters in that section exploring important concepts that flesh out that particular core teaching.

The final section of the book is entitled "A Post-Nicene Christianity" and examines the implications of these five teachings and a possible direction for Christian faith in the 21st century.

It is my sincere hope that you will find this exploration as liberating and as exhilarating as it has been and continues to be for me. For those of you who are persons of faith, I hope this deepens your journey into the mystery of Jesus and the Divine. If you are struggling with the Christian faith or have left it, I hope that this in some small way might provide a path to embrace it once again.

PART I:
FIVE CORE TEACHINGS

CHAPTER 2:
READING WITH A SECOND NAÏVETÉ

Who in the world wants to be naïve? Lord knows I don't, and when I think about it I'm hard pressed to think of anyone I know who wants to be thought of in that way, or worse to actually be that. Naïve people are primitive, easily duped, choose a world of fantasy over reality, and are often mistaken about how things really work. Put harshly, for most of us naïve people are seen as the modern equivalent of the village idiot. And so I ask again, who in their right mind would want to be naïve?

As this chapter's title implies, however, that is just what I am suggesting. But I'm not suggesting the kind of naïveté described above, but rather something altogether different, a developed or "second" naïveté. To understand what a second naïveté is, however, we need to take an honest look at why we think being naïve is a bad thing and what we might mean by a first, or original, naïveté.

The 20th-century philosopher and theologian Paul Ricoeur, in an important book titled *The Symbolism of Evil*, outlined how we as modern people have been so heavily shaped by the intellectual and philosophical ideas of the Enlightenment. He argues, and I will outline shortly, that because of our almost universal acceptance of understanding the world in strictly rational and scientific ways we are no longer capable of engaging the Bible the way our ancestors did. This doesn't mean that the Enlightenment was a bad thing in itself, but instead that we are prone to look at very different things than did our ancestors when we read scripture, and as a consequence find it difficult (or even impossible) in our search for meaning to read scripture simply as a story. Ricoeur doesn't argue—nor do I—that we should return to a pre-Enlightenment way of thinking. Nor does he, or I, argue that we abandon everything that science and reason have given us. But if we are to know anything of the Jesus who inspired the Gospels it is essential that we recover something of the practice and deep knowledge that was accessible to our pre-Enlightenment ancestors. Ricoeur calls this approach, reading with a "second naïveté."

THE ENLIGHTENMENT AND ITS EFFECT

It's hard for us to imagine how people who lived before the middle of the 17th century understood the Bible. How we think as contemporary people and how we understand the Bible owes itself heavily to the intellectual and philosophical developments of the Renaissance and the Enlightenment. It is from these periods of intellectual growth and development that we get the rationalism of people like René Descartes, Baruch Spinoza, Gottfried Leibniz, and Immanuel Kant; the humanism of Desiderius Erasmus, Niccolo Machiavelli, and Thomas More; the liberalism of John Locke and Adam Smith; and the empiricism of Francis Bacon, Thomas Hobbes, John Locke and David Hume. And while all of those names might not be familiar to everyone, the ideas they came up with are at the heart of how we think today about everything.

Because of these thinkers we imagine our world and ourselves in a very different way than did our ancestors. It would be hard to find a person today who doesn't accept the importance of observation and the connection between measurable data and verifiable truth. Moreover, concepts of the mind and the body are shaped by a material understanding of reality that is rooted in the scientific language of observation and measurement (i.e., empiricism) and a mental understanding of reality that is rooted in the psychological language of self awareness and internal thought process (i.e., rationalism).

The ways in which the Bible is studied that arose in the Renaissance and flowered in the Enlightenment owe their origins to these same intellectual movements. For most of the history of Western Christianity it was generally known that the books of the New Testament had originally been written in Greek and that the books of the Old Testament had originally been written in Hebrew. But prior to the 16th century there was general agreement throughout Europe that the Latin translation of the Bible attributed to St. Jerome (the Vulgate) was authoritative and beyond question. In other words, it was assumed that while there were noticeable "variances" between different Greek and Hebrew manuscripts, the texts in the Vulgate were believed to be, without question, the correct version.

But as rational inquiry and scientific application began to gain traction within the intellectual communities of Europe, the Bible could not remain immune to their influence. Ultimately philosophers, historians, biblical scholars and finally theologians began to apply the methods of rational inquiry and observation to the Bible. This application of scientific principals to the Bible became known commonly as "biblical criticism" (meaning to take a rational and empirical look at scripture). Known biblical manuscripts in ancient Greek and Hebrew were examined for variations between the two, while at the same time methods of observation and measurement were developed to argue for the authenticity of one version over the other. From these methods alone much was learned about the texts of the Bible and a deep appreciation for the very human nature of the texts began to develop.

Ultimately, by the end of the 19th century, from the application of scientific methods and rational thought, biblical criticism had developed into a broad group of scholarly techniques that attempted to, among other things, examine biblical texts for errors that crept into the manuscript tradition, search for the sources which lie behind biblical texts, examine the form of any given section of text for its meaning and its origin, examine how the individual portions of a text are put together to create meaning, and examine biblical texts in terms of the author's intended message or as a piece of literature.

In the midst of this development the institutional church (both Catholic and Protestant) in different places and at different times resisted the insights that arose from these methods. The arguments against these methods initially appealed to more ancient models of thought, but ultimately no one was immune to the larger intellectual movement afoot, and by the end of the 19th century it was rare to hear arguments against the insights of biblical criticism that weren't equally framed from the assumptions of science and reason.

Even modern fundamentalism relies on principles that come from the intellectual and philosophical language of the Enlightenment. While fundamentalism argues that its approach to the Bible is more in keeping with ancient tradition, this model of interpretation equally has its roots in the assumptions of rationalism and empiricism. For example, it is often argued by fundamentalists that the Bible has a "plain" meaning, which is intended to convey that we can read the Bible because the meaning of the words contained within it are self-evident.

You may be surprised to learn that an assumption that the Bible is self-evident would have been alien to pre-Enlightenment thinkers. Instead, before the Renaissance, it was generally understood that the meaning of the Bible could only be known through the inspiration of the Holy Spirit, which came almost exclusively through the teaching and instruction of the Church.

So the argument that language is self-evident assumes that words have meaning in themselves apart from culture and that we, through our rational minds, can connect to that meaning. In other words, language is seen as an expression of consciousness that can be universally accessed through rational process. This heavy reliance on reason and language is at the heart of rationalist thought.[1]

The other pattern often found in fundamentalist thought is the use of the Bible as a proof text for reality. In other words, the interpretation or understanding of human experience is weighed against the "evidence" of scripture. It is presumed by the fundamentalist reader that the text is an empirical document recording events in observable and measurable ways that can then be used as a "test bed" for further observation. In other words, scripture is held out as an observational proof of the existence of any number of faith-based claims. When looked at from a historical perspective, we can quickly see that this is actually a misapplication of empiricism in regard to a text, but nonetheless an attempt to place the empirical norms of science onto scripture.

So regardless of whether fundamentalists consciously accept rational and empirical methods, it is clear that modern fundamentalism is thoroughly shaped by the very intellectual models against which it argues.

Ultimately, whether we choose to be aware of it or not, humanity's understanding of the world—and consequentially its understanding of scripture—has been permanently changed by a general acceptance of observational technique and rational inquiry that has its roots first in the Renaissance and ultimately in the Enlightenment.

The current abundance of books and essays that examine biblical texts from a critically rational and observational perspective show just how common and accepted the model has become. We don't need to look very hard at the local bookstore or online to find literally hundreds of books dedicated to finding the "historical Jesus," exposing the "lost" Gospels, or talking about the movement from the person of Jesus to the theological idea of Christ. Even popular works of fiction, like Dan Brown's *The Da Vinci Code* ultimately owe their existence to the work of scholars engaged in biblical criticism. And, while much energy, sweat, and even blood continues to be shed inside the life of the institutional church, increasingly many people are finding little compelling from these arguments or their insights. Or as one young adult once said to me, "All of that stuff is interesting, but it's not much more than brain candy." The truth is that the fights that consume institutional religion are absurd and irrelevant to the real issues of most people's day-to-day lives.

This is not to say that biblical criticism has had no value or is a "lost cause." On the contrary, although there remain some fundamentalist elements within contemporary Christianity that would argue otherwise, the development of biblical criticism and its ongoing growth in the centuries that followed has led to a level of biblical understanding that never existed before. It has freed us from unhelpful superstition, allowed us to authentically embrace the complexity of the origins of Christianity as a religion, given us the opportunity to recognize that the question of truth in regard to the content of the Bible is not simple, and helped us to realize that the truths we discover are not always universal.

Ironically, as we struggle with a lack of inspiration from an Enlightenment approach to scripture, we also tend to regard our pre-Enlightenment ancestors as intellectually primitive or backward because of the implicit assumptions in our culture today, and we tend to regard any process of thought that isn't scientific or rational as suspect. We might argue that, in light of how well those modes of thought have served humanity, we are well justified in our disregard. And, while we might concede that point in some ways, it doesn't mean that rationalism and empiricism are perfect. Our almost exclusively rational and scientific approach has its limitations. And without some appropriate respect for other models of thinking we are at grave risk of misunderstanding our ancestors and ourselves.

How exactly did people read and understand the Bible before the rise of these other ways of thinking? What was at the heart of their understanding? What can we learn from their approach?

READING WITH A FIRST NAÏVETÉ

It is not hard to agree with the idea that people before the Enlightenment were no more or less naïve than any other group of human beings. Just as today, there were likely naïve people and "worldly" people in the medieval and ancient worlds. If this were not the case how would we have the great thinkers from ancient Greece and Rome like Archimedes, Pythagoras, Plato, Aristotle, Plutarch, and Livy? Moreover how could such realities as the Roman Empire, the culture of classical Greece, and the wonders of ancient Egypt exist if everyone before the Enlightenment were simply naïve?

Again we have to be clear about what we mean when we refer to pre-Enlightenment thinkers as being those who come out of a "first naïveté." In this case we are simply saying that the rational and empirical assumptions we presume in all inquiry were not present.

This is not to say that ancient peoples couldn't think rationally or that observation and measurement didn't play a role in their lives, but the meaning and place of those concepts did not inform their whole sense of reality. What we take to be the "really real" was only a part of their reality.

It may be hard to imagine, but before the 16th century, it was common to believe multiple things at face value, even when they contradicted one another. Pretty much anything could be accepted if it reflected the truth of lived experience. Because of this, people like the ancient philosophers of Greece were able to engage the material world in ways that we would recognize as scientific, while at the same time holding to a literal belief in the gods of the Greek pantheon. In the ancient mind there was no conflict, because science and religion each represented a different dimension of reality, and to ignore any source of truth was to miss out on important insights about the nature and meaning of existence.

Before the Enlightenment, stories served as a way of exploring and sharing the truth of lived experience. Some stories were presented as history in the way we understand that word today. Other stories were accepted to be what we might call fiction, but they were nonetheless accepted as completely true because they expressed something that was considered an important dimension of human experience. Whether history, biography, or fiction, stories like these were plentiful in the pre-Enlightenment world. We often are quick to discount them as make-believe or wishful thinking. But to ancient peoples they were something very different. When a story conveyed truth it was often referred to by the classical Greek word for story, *mythos,* or "myth." These myths were not understood simply as made-up stories to serve as a metaphor or allegory for truth, but rather they were accepted at face value as being true in every sense.

Today we hear the word myth and we often presume immediately that it is not true. We assume that myths are fantastical creations of the imagination with little connection to reality. Our modern imagination boggles at the idea that a myth is true, but for ancient peoples this wasn't even a question. Much like children today accept the literal reality of Santa Claus and the Easter Bunny for a time in their lives, stories about the place and nature of the Divine were understood in a literal way because they did more than point to deep truth. Children accept the reality of a fat man in a red suit and a six-foot bunny who hides eggs because they do more than point to truth. They express deeply true experiences. If these myths of Christmas and Easter didn't reflect the truth of a lived experience, then most children wouldn't believe, even at a very young age. But instead, children experience Santa, the Easter Bunny, the Tooth Fairy, and countless other childhood myths as very deep truths of human experience. We, as adults, perpetuate those myths not to delude our children, but because on some level (perhaps unconscious at times) we continue to recognize the deep value of the truths to which they point.

The ancient mind was no different in this regard. For ancient peoples, myths were accepted because of the truth they contained. There was no need to reconcile the witness of observation and measurement to a story in order to accept it as true, nor was there any need to reconcile the rational inconsistencies within that story since those inconsistencies were, often quite literally, immaterial.

Likewise, sources of truth, like the Bible, were accepted as story and taken at face value. For the ancient person there is no need to question what of the Gospels are actually the words of Jesus and what in the text is placed there by some later scribe or theologian, because the text is not approached with those questions in mind. To do so would be like coming at the Santa story wanting to know the origin of the myth and whether or not it had been "corrupted" by some later tradition. While there might be some interesting insights that come from such an inquiry it contains none of the wisdom, wonder, or meaning that simply engaging the myth brings. And so most of us would, if confronted by such an approach on Christmas morning, wonder what child or adult in their right mind would even consider such a thing. But even as we accept myths like Santa and the Easter Bunny, we are unwilling to suspend our disbelief forever. We all grow up and come to know that neither Santa nor the Easter Bunny is "real" in any tangible way.

This is the basic tension between the first naïveté and our current way of thinking. We value the truth of reason and scientific inquiry, but find ourselves yearning for meaning and inspiration. We recognize the value of myth, but have relegated it away from reality, leaving it devoid of its power to speak to the substance of our lives.

READING WITH A SECOND NAÏVETÉ

For those of us living today, neither a wholly mythical orientation nor a strictly rational and scientific one is sufficient. If there is going to be any hope of finding meaning in our lives, a third alternative for exploring spiritual matters is needed. I believe that Paul Ricoeur offers a reasonable approach by suggesting that we consider reading the scriptures with a "second naïveté." The path to such a method, however, requires us to accept some truths and redefine a couple of important concepts.

First, let's review some truths that are inescapable for anyone living in a modern or post-modern context. To start, we can never claim to read the Bible or any other religious text with a childlike innocence or, even more, the way that a pre-Enlightenment thinker did. Next, we must accept that we are so steeped in the assumptions of rationalism and empiricism that we can never break free from them (and likely wouldn't want to anyway). And finally, we must accept that because of the critical nature of our thought and our insistence on reality being defined by rational thought and verifiable experience we, more often than not, have skepticism towards scripture and religious ideas that our ancestors could not have imagined. Having said that, there is a way forward. And its path involves symbol and story.

As we've already explored earlier in this chapter, because of these truths we are never going to be able to simply read the Bible and accept the stories contained there at face value. If we are forced to accept these stories as empirically true, then we're already dead in the water and might as well not bother moving forward. But what if, instead, we chose to simply treat these stories as stories. In other words, what if we chose to treat the Bible as literature, recognizing that it contains language that points to the truth of human experience. To do so would free us from having to reconcile exaggerated claims and miraculous stories to what we know to be true about the Universe.

For example, even though the Bible presumes that the whole Universe can be understood in terms of the Earth being a flat disc with a dome above (the sky) and a dome below (the underworld) and heaven is what exists above and outside the dome, we are free to read the story knowing the truth of the Universe as science has revealed it without having to translate that reality into the story we are reading or vice versa. By doing this we are not setting aside anything that rational or scientific thought conveys; we are simply respecting the integrity of the story in its own context.

Recognizing that these stories are written to convey the truth of human experience, however, also requires us to recognize that, while there may be understandings of reality that do not mesh with ours, the stories are written to convey the truth of a lived experience that may still have relevance to human experience today.

To access the truth of those experiences it is important to take the time to recognize what language, metaphors, and images in the story serve as symbols pointing beyond the immediate message in the story to something that rises above ordinary day-to-day life. In many cases this may be where God language and miracle serve a purpose, but not always. It is just as possible that the stories purported to be parables told by Jesus serve a similar purpose. As a post-modern person, a small voice in me is saying in response, "That's all well and good, but why would I choose symbols over what's real? I mean aren't symbols just indirect substitutes for something we'd be better off understanding directly?"

Yes and no. Sometimes we use the word symbol to describe an image or word that simply points to something else. In those cases, a better way to describe such a function is to call it a "sign." Just like street signs, signs point the way to something. When something serves as a sign it usually only has meaning in terms of what it points to. We sometimes use signs to point to things we don't know or understand (e.g., using the sign "∞" to mean "infinity"). More often than not we use signs to point to something we know (e.g., when we see the logo "Crest" we know we're buying toothpaste).

Symbols, however, are more than signs. Because they do more than point to something else, they usually have meaning of their own and they bring meaning to the thing they point to. In other words, symbols actually participate in what they are pointing to. There are lots of examples of how we continue to use symbolic language even in our post-modern context. An example from secular life that comes to mind immediately is the American flag.

From the perspective of sign we could say that the American flag is a sign of the nation of the United States of America. And in one very real sense, we would be correct. But the American flag has taken on enormous meaning of its own over the last two centuries and so now it serves not only to point to the nation, but also to inform us what that nation is. Within an American context, the flag often stands as an embodiment of liberty, justice, or democracy, and serves either to reinforce those values in American life or to critique the lack of them. At the same time, in some foreign contexts, the American flag can stand as an embodiment of imperialism, foreign aggression, or economic oppression, and can serve either to galvanize anti-American attitudes or justify rejecting a particular culture or way of living.

This is just one example of the presence and power of symbol in our life today, which speaks volumes to us in ways that a simple surface meaning of language cannot.

Because of the obvious irrationality and lack of sustainable scientific proof of much of the Bible, we have become suspicious or outright skeptical of the stories it contains. But if we can recognize that much of that language can be freed from its literal bondage through an appropriate recognition of its symbolic value, we are then free to embrace the stories of the Bible as mythic literature and uncover the lost wisdom of ancient voices. In the voices and vision of the ancient biblical scribes we can find through their stories and symbols a deep sense of inspiration and meaning. It is from this frame that we will look at the Gospels in the next chapter.

CHAPTER 3:
THE SHAPE OF A LIFE LIVED

Thanks to centuries of scientific and rational examination of the Bible we now know that there isn't a single text in it that doesn't have multiple versions depending on which scribe copied the text. We also know that even when there is consistency in the copying there are many texts, which represent more than one way of thinking about whatever the text is presenting. Finally, in the case of the Gospels, not only do we have the variations outlined above, but we also have differences, sometimes significant and sometimes conflicting, between the way each of the Gospels represents the life, message, and meaning of Jesus. And so it begs the question, how can we, with any certainty, know anything about Jesus or his life?

If anything is clear, it is that the Gospels, regardless of intention, serve a lot of different purposes, and those purposes come from a lot of different people. Each author, and subsequently each scribe who copied the text, had more than one agenda in what they wrote. Variations between the four Gospels and between different manuscripts of those Gospels make this abundantly clear. But, what makes things even more complex is that each of us brings any number of filters, projections, and agendas when we read the Gospels. As I mentioned in chapter 1 about my own journey, we don't simply derive our images of Jesus from these texts; we also have images that come from our own unique histories, languages, and cultures. In those moments when I am especially conscious of this reality I find it amazing that we can, at this point, agree on anything about the person of Jesus of Nazareth.

What all of this means, however, is that the Gospels cannot be reduced to any one category. For each of us these texts may well serve as history, theology, spirituality, literature, mythology, or liturgy (worship text). It also means that these texts have served, at any given time, as justification for a whole host of behaviors that may or may not be present in the text. And, even when they are, may have little to do with the reasoning behind the behavior they are being used to justify.

One particularly unsavory example of such a usage would be slavery in the United States prior to the Civil War. Even the most cursory reading of the Bible shows that slavery was an accepted reality for the peoples and cultures represented in the Bible. This isn't really a surprise, since slavery was a part of the norms of most ancient cultures and was one of the consequences of military conquest. The method of slavery found in 19th-century North America, however, had little in common with the models of slavery found in the ancient world. Racially based slavery, which displaced large numbers of African peoples, was based on the assumption of the inferiority of those peoples and implanted a set of racist beliefs that continue to infect American culture to this day. The assumption of the biological inferiority of the enslaved found in the racist attitudes that justified slavery in the 19th century would be alien to ancient peoples. Nonetheless, despite the obvious differences between the two models of servitude, proponents of slavery felt perfectly justified in using biblical texts to justify the perpetuation of racially based slavery.

The point here is that whenever we presume to talk about what the Bible has to say, or moreover to teach its meaning, we must be very careful to be aware about what we are projecting into the text and what may or may not actually be present in it. To some degree it is likely impossible to completely avoid some level of projection, but to the degree we can, we should make it a priority to avoid projecting our own assumptions, values, images, and culture into the text.

Having said that, we are still left with the quandary of what, if any, meaning do the Gospels hold for those of us living in the early part of the 21st century. Are these simply relics of an ancient superstition or do they contain wisdom that can still bring meaning and a sense of purpose to our lives? I believe they can. But to do so, we must approach them with the second naïveté we discussed in the last chapter. When we do, an amazing dimension is revealed that allows us to see something that up to this point may have been invisible.

If we look at the four Gospels contained in the New Testament, without the benefit of scholarship and with as few of our presumptions as possible, what we find are four stories that tell us something about the life and death of a first-century Palestinian man. They share with us what each writer believes to be the salient facts of this man's life. And, they share how they understood the meaning and the purpose of that life.

These stories, however, are not biographies. In every case large portions of the man's life are omitted and many of the details about him that we might expect in a biography are either given little attention or glossed over. For example, while we can find stories of birth and childhood they are quite few and most of his childhood and early adult life are missing. Further, while we hear in these narratives many stories about Jesus being followed and seen, there is not a single description of what he looked like.

So, it is clear that the people who wrote these stories were not interested in writing biographies of Jesus of Nazareth. Instead they seem to be quite focused on the last three years of his life and a specific set of events that occurred within that time frame. Is this because they didn't know anything else? Possibly. But perhaps the reason the other details are missing is because that information does not serve the purpose that these texts intend to serve.

Again, reading without the filter of scholarship and with as little presumption as possible, it seems that what we have in these four narratives is not biography, but something altogether different. Each of these texts shares what it believes to be the most important dimensions of what Jesus taught and how Jesus lived. In fact, it seems clear that much effort is given to show the congruence between these two realities. Even when there are miracle stories, those events are included in order to solidify the congruence of life and teaching.

From a modern perspective then, we might refer to these stories as portraying the "ethic" of Jesus. It is this ethic that then forms the foundation for making sense out of his life and death and leads to support the assertions made regarding the ongoing power and presence of his life. As the South African biblical theologian, Gerald O. West, puts it, these texts represent not simply biography, philosophy, or theology, but are a presentation of "the shape of a life lived."

This means that the Gospels represent the experience of a group of people who knew Jesus. It also means that they represent an invitation to share in the experience of those who knew Jesus.

Much scholarship has been done to help us understand the theological and cultural thinking of the authors of the Gospels. Furthermore, with the discovery of the "lost" gospels in places like Nag Hammadi, Egypt, we have come to understand that there were a variety of ways of philosophically and theologically understanding the meaning and purpose of Jesus' life and death beyond what is presented in the four Gospels of the New Testament.

Our purpose is not to explore or debate much of the metaphysical meaning that continues to divide and conflict the church. Rather, it is to acknowledge the nature of the text from a second naïveté. It is to see, namely, that the four texts we find in the New Testament represent the shape of a human life. That this human life, attached to the person of Jesus of Nazareth, was sufficiently compelling to inspire persons to perpetuate his pattern and the teaching associated with it. And that, both in the life of Jesus and in the congruent patterning of their own lives, they experienced something of the Divine again and again. In fact, I would argue that they experienced, first in the presence of Jesus and then in their own lives as they mimicked his pattern, a direct and tangible connection to the Divine. Why else would anyone take the time to preserve his teachings and be so selective in the presentation of his life?

While we are not going to focus on them beyond this point, it is worth noting that many of the other Gospels that did not make it into the New Testament follow a similar pattern. People, then and now, find the shape of this first-century Palestinian's life inspiring and compelling, even when they do not find the supernatural elements of the story believable.

CHAPTER 4:
TEACHING, SUTRA, AND KÖAN

WHICH JESUS DO YOU PICTURE?

As a child my image of Jesus was of a kind and gentle big brother who looked like the people I knew, and talked like the people I knew. By the time I was 20 I had gained enough sophistication to recognize that Jesus spoke Aramaic, lived in ancient Palestine, and practiced an ancient form of Judaism, but nonetheless I still imagined him as this gentle man who would be as comfortable in my context as he was in his own. I also had become familiar at that point with the bulk of the Gospels and saw him as a moral teacher, as self-aware of his divinity, and who, by engaging in miraculous acts, proved that he was divine. By the end of seminary at the age of 30, I had come to see Jesus even more in his Palestinian context and recognized the rich traditions that revolved around him from those who wrote the Gospels. And while I was more than willing to accept that many of the miracles were likely symbolic rather than literal, I still saw him basically as this deeply compassionate and kind moral teacher and as a divine savior who delivered us from the debt of our sins.

My point in telling this little narrative is to emphasize that throughout, in what was a very subconscious process, the basic image of Jesus I had formed in my childhood never really left. Moreover, that image shaped every image I had subsequently. Scholarship and data could enhance my image of Jesus. It could challenge it, and/or expand it, but the founding image formed in my early childhood had a durability that persisted throughout.

Are any of us are much different? One of the great challenges that face anyone who goes searching after Jesus is that it is virtually impossible to find him without bringing along our own projections and assumptions. Depending on the images, metaphors, and values we attain over the years, each of us has a tendency to see only a particular view of Jesus. And not just any particular view, but one shaped by the norms, values, and images of the culture within which we live. It is by this point that this chapter is informed.

No one would likely disagree with the statement that Jesus was a first-century Palestinian Jew, but is that what we imagine when we think of Jesus? Or are there a variety of messages, images, and cultural metaphors that blend together as an amalgam to form a vision that may, or may not, have anything to do with the man behind the name?

One of the greatest challenges to my prejudices of Jesus of Nazareth (both positive and negative) was exposure to the work of biblical scholars who explore the historical context within which Jesus lived.[2] Further challenge came when I began to look at Judaism not through the filter of Christianity, but as a religion in its own right whose mystical ways of understanding life and the Universe look far more Eastern than Western in their presuppositions.[3] And then finally, the last of the challenges to my assumptions of Jesus came from the history of the development of the church. This history revealed explicitly how the understandings of Jesus and his teaching shifted as the role of the church shifted (sometimes subtly) with each successive culture over the last two millennia.

It would likely be no great surprise to anyone to realize that not only do fashion and politics change over time, but so does language. Words, when they survive, often have meaning that shifts, sometimes dramatically. For example, in the present context if we were going to convey that something was positively spectacular, we might describe it as "awesome." However, just a mere 150 years ago the word that would have been used to express that experience would have been "awful," implying that the experience was literally "full of awe."

While we may appreciate the sophistication of such a word study, we have no intention of trying to convince anyone in the present context that the current use of awful as a negative connotation is incorrect. But, a contemporary person reading a text from the 1750s may well misunderstand the author if they are unaware of the meaning of the word in that context. If such simple "translation" errors are possible in our own language within a culture out of which our own has developed, imagine just how much more difficult it is to comprehend an author's intent when reading a text that is, quite literally in most regards, alien to the language and culture within which we find ourselves today.

This brings into sharp focus the difficulty one faces when looking at the shape of the life of Jesus and his teachings as presented in the Gospel texts of the Bible. I have become increasingly convinced that the Jesus we think we know and see (both those of us who are devoted to him and those of us who would challenge his existence or his teaching) has little to do with the man who existed. But, this is not the fault of the authors of the Gospel texts. Rather it is the tragic, but understandable, issue of projection, mistranslation, and misinterpretation inherent in the task of trying to reach back nearly two millennia.

Accordingly, before being able to look at the teachings of Jesus we must first take a look at our own cultural assumptions about teaching and from where they come.

A WESTERN VIEW OF TEACHING

The whole notion of teaching in the West has its origins in models established in classical Greece many centuries before the Common

Era.[4] The Macedonians, who produced Alexander the Great, adopted these patterns and spread them throughout his empire. Further, they were adopted by the Romans and became a normative part of Roman life and culture, spreading with them to every corner of that empire. Even after the fall and decline of the Western Roman Empire, much of the classical model of education (to the degree that it could be) was maintained in the monasteries of Western Europe and laid the foundation for the educational models of most modern Western nations.

A number of presuppositions lie at the heart of Western models of teaching that deserve to be made explicit. Our purpose here is not to be exhaustive of the Western approach or to make any judgments about these presuppositions, but to make a number of core assumptions explicit so that when we look at an Eastern approach (of which Judaism is a part) we can then be clear about how they differ.

1. Western models tend to focus on individual identity.

Western rational thought is best summed up in the words of the French philosopher, René Descartes, when he famously articulated, *"Cogito ergo sum,"* ("I think, therefore I am."). In the West the experience of an internal voice within the mind has led to the assumption that each of us is a separate unit upon whose existence no others are required. This does not mean that we do not recognize the importance of the other in terms of our survival or the betterment of our experience, but our being/consciousness is not dependent upon any other being or consciousness. This basic supposition is projected on the whole of the natural Universe, resulting in the understanding that each perceivable object is separate and independent. To put it in other words, we and everything else travel this world as separate atoms occasionally bumping into one another, colliding for good or ill.

2. Western models tend to a mechanistic worldview.

Starting as early as the Greek physicists of the 5th century BCE[5] there was a separation between the internal life and that of the discernible world. Through methods of observation and measurement and development of theories of function these early thinkers led to the full development of philosophical thought in Greece, which flowered in the thinking of both Plato and Aristotle. And while all of these philosophies accepted the reality of a spiritual (or dare we say psychological) dimension they also asserted that there was equally a separate physical dimension in which we lived that functioned by its own rules. Whether by looking at the mathematics of Pythagoras, the geometry of Archimedes, or the natural sciences of Zeno we see regularly the assumption of a mechanical universe that operates by natural laws.

3. Western models are based on the assumption of the inevitability of conflict.

By looking at early writings from the classical period or later Western Christian writings, it becomes clear that the prevailing assumption is that all of life can be understood as being about a basic tension between soul and body (desire), God and Satan, or (to put it in more generic terms) good and evil. Using such a dichotomy sets up an assumption that the goal of every action is victory (e.g., find a problem, find a solution), and that every action or lack thereof has moral consequence (e.g., productive is good, non-productive is bad). It also assumes that every action is marked by conflict between that which is good and that which is bad. Even when the conflict is so small that it is not noticed, it is nonetheless there.

4. Western models tend to focus on the ideal.

Of all the core concepts, the idea that Western models tend to focus upon concepts of the ideal is the easiest to see once made explicit. One need merely look to the writings of Plato and Aristotle to see this. Whether we are talking about Plato's notion of eternal forms, or Aristotle's idea of the unmoved mover, we see repeatedly from that point forward an appeal to an ideal as the motivation for all inquiry and action. Even in a post-Enlightenment reality there is a constant temptation to skew the data to fit an ideal. History is replete with examples of scientific models, which were based on the presumption of an immutable truth only later to be disproven after much resistance. For specific examples one need merely look at the variety of elaborate mechanical models invented to "prove" the centrality of the Earth in the solar system.

AN EASTERN VIEW OF TEACHING

Unlike in the West, the pursuit of knowledge in the East had a different understanding and followed a different model altogether. Built upon the teachings of sacred texts (Torah, Bhagavad Gita, the Dharma of the Buddha, the Tao Te Ching), these philosophies do not reflect the assumptions of models dominant in the West. Below are the corollary points from an Eastern viewpoint. Again, this outline is not meant to be exhaustive or designed to make judgments about these assumptions, but to simply outline them for the sake of comparison.

1. Eastern models tend to focus on communal identity.

An examination of the Hebrew scriptures, the Gospels, and teachings of the Bhagavad Gita or those of the Dharma will reveal patterns of knowledge and self that are wholly bound up in the concept of community. And, while much is spoken of the individual, it is always understood to be in the context of a communal identity. In Judaism, the importance of community is expressed in the idea that even the Divine is known from within a communal context (e.g., "I am the God of your ancestors. The God of Abraham, Isaac, and Jacob."). Whereas in Buddhism, Buddhist teaching (the Dharma) is almost always passed through communal transmission (the Sangha). In an Eastern model the idea of a wholly private, individual, and personal faith is alien.

2. Eastern models tend to an organic worldview.

In the Hebrew scriptures the interconnectedness of life is presumed from the start. In fact, there is no divide between mind, soul, and body. Words for emotions point to parts of the body and much of the rules that govern the practice of one's faith are overtly mundane and rooted in the "stuff" of life. Similarly in other Eastern practices the world is seen in its varied expressions as being part of an organic whole out of which all life develops and much of Eastern religious practice is learning to honor, respect, and live in harmony with the whole while transcending the differences.

3. Eastern models are based on harmony as a principal motivation.

Whether looking at the early Christian community, the Torah principals of community found in Leviticus, the urgings of Siddhartha Gautama (the founder of Buddhism) toward mutual respect, those of Confucius emphasizing harmony and working together for the good of the whole, or the Hindu path of love (Bhakti Yoga) which emphasizes the Bhagavad Gita's teachings on harmony and mutuality, one finds frequently in the Eastern context a focus on the belief that harmony is itself a core motivation for human existence and a model for communal living.

4. Eastern models tend to be pragmatic rather than ideal.

In the 21st century we tend to think of pragmatism as being about practicality, but it is, in fact, about something quite different altogether. To be pragmatic rather than ideal is to be concerned about what is true, rather than what should be true. It is with this understanding of the word pragmatic that we can say that Eastern models tend to be pragmatic rather than ideal. In Judaism the tradition of law and custom captured in the Torah does not hold humanity to an ideal, but instead deals with the truth of the situation of human living and sets boundaries for that living. The Buddhist assumption of suffering arising out of attachment is not an idealized reality, but an experience to which anyone can relate. In these models there is no ideal humanity to which we are striving, but only the struggling reality and the need to respond.

LESSON, SUTRA, AND KÖAN

It's not hard to see, in light of all that we've just explored, that in the West a teaching is basically understood as a set of rational statements that can be transmitted, understood, and mastered. In fact, it might even be argued that a teaching is an object of knowledge that a teacher imparts to the student through the mechanical process of teaching.

The Eastern concepts of *sutra* and *köan* are, in a Western context, likewise often translated as "teaching." This is technically correct, but if we do not take into account what we have just outlined, we are in significant danger of missing the deeper meaning of those words and projecting our Western assumptions upon them.

The word sutra means "string" and reflects the holistic approach of an Eastern mindset. Rather than simply being an object of knowledge that can be mechanically transmitted, sutra represents a string (theme) of truth, which has unplumbable depths into which one can be invited. This notion of string often implies story and many of these "teachings" are conveyed within the context of a story. There is a proverb from Zen Buddhism attributed to Siddhartha Gautama that exemplifies the notion of sutra:

> A student came to the master one day and asked him, "Master, what did you do before you achieved enlightenment?"
> The master replied, "I chopped wood and carried water."
> The student then asked the master, "What do you do now that you are enlightened?"

The master replied, "Now that I am enlightened, I chop wood and I carry water."

The story itself is not a teaching in the Western sense, but rather is an invitation into the wisdom contained within the story. This begs the reader to ask questions and explore first the story and then the reader's own self. For example: (1) Is it that nothing has changed except enlightenment? (2) Is it that the master is now fully present to chopping wood and carrying water, as he was not before? Or (3) is it that what one does is immaterial to enlightenment? Perhaps each one is correct in its own context, perhaps none, perhaps all are true at the same time. Perhaps there are questions, which only arise as we wrestle further with the story.

An exception to the story model comes from Zen Buddhism that uses an additional word for its exception. This word köan is also often translated as teaching but like sutra makes none of the assumptions of the West.

A köan may or may not come in the context of a sutra or story, but is nonetheless an invitation into mystery and the holistic reality of any particular pursuit of knowledge. Köans use as their principal medium paradox and absurdity. A quintessential example of a Buddhist köan is, "What is the sound of one hand clapping?" or even more popular, "If a tree falls in the forest and no one is there, does it make a sound?"

By asking questions that have no definitive answer the reader is left to explore the paradox, and by doing so to explore the mystery of existence. As we can see this approach is quite different from that of a Western approach to knowledge.

JESUS: A TEACHER OF LESSONS OR ONE WHO OFFERS SUTRAS?

All of this then begs the question: Just what sort of teacher was Jesus? For much of the history of Western Christianity the answer would have been that Jesus was a teacher of lessons (i.e., discreet truths of God and humanity meant to improve the life of the reader/listener). But in light of the overtly Eastern components of Judaism, is that really a fair thing to assert, or have we been too quick to project our Western ideas onto this very Eastern first-century Palestinian? Perhaps an examination of Jesus' teaching models, as reported in the Gospels, would be helpful.

One of the difficulties we have when trying to examine Jesus' teaching model is that it has become normative to see every aspect of Jesus' life as instruction. While this may be perfectly valid as a spiritual discipline, it is not particularly helpful for us. I believe that what is more worthwhile to examine are his explicit moments of teaching identified in the Gospels as such, and the things he said and did which clearly are shared in the literary context of the Gospels as a teaching moment. These put together should help us to see clearly whether or not Jesus taught from a predominantly Eastern or Western perspective.

Parable - Jesus Told Stories

Depending on how one numbers them, there are somewhere between 44 and 46 parables in the Gospels (i.e., 44-46 instances when Jesus opted to tell a story as a means of teaching).[6] Put simply, this means that Jesus was, first and foremost, a storyteller. He didn't simply tell stories to entertain, but rather to invite people into concepts that were larger than any direct statement could contain. Further, while it was clear that these stories were serving as allegory or metaphor, rarely did he provide an explanation for their meaning. Instead, again and again, he left the interpretation up to the listener/reader allowing for the teaching to be an entry into deeper truth and mystery.

Action - Jesus Modeled Behavior

Jesus didn't just teach through words. He lived, and as such how he lived was important to him. As stated in the previous chapter the behavior of Jesus reported in the Gospels reflects a congruity with what Jesus said and how he taught. Jesus didn't just teach peace; he lived peace. He didn't just teach justice; he lived justice. He didn't just teach compassion; he lived compassion. And all of these things (peace, justice, compassion, and many others) weren't ideals to be lived up to, but realities to be embraced.

Paradox and Exaggeration - Jesus made statements that challenge rational thought

Jesus made statements that were, both in his own context and now, outrageous. An examination of the Gospels reveals multiple uses of exaggeration and hyperbole regularly. Whether referring to Peter as Satan, inviting us to pluck out an eye, or to "let the dead bury the dead," Jesus used exaggerated language as a means of startling the listener/reader and inviting a reframing of reality into a place mystery and discovery.

Jesus: A Jewish Wisdom Teacher

When we see just how much Jesus comes out of a model of storytelling and the use of paradox, we begin to see him more in the stream of Eastern than Western thought. It is in this light that he looks much more like a wisdom teacher, rather than simply a conveyer of a morality code. It is also from this vantage that we begin to recognize that, while each of his teachings can be discussed discretely, there is also the possibility that there are larger themes at work in his teaching that are worthy of our attention.

Because the teaching of Jesus is unplumbable, it would be arrogant to presume that there are only five themes in the Gospels. On the contrary there are many, many more and a wealth of writing already on a number of them. But from this point in the book we shift our attention to the five themes that have arisen for me repeatedly throughout my journey with these texts.

And, while reference to scripture will be a part of our exploration, it will only be one component on the journey through the rest of the book. Along the way we will move through the cultural assumptions that have shaped us, the insights of modern inquiry, and the challenges that Jesus raises for us in these Gospel themes (i.e., sutras).

CHAPTER 5:
A SUMMARY OF THE FIVE SUTRAS OF JESUS

As a preacher and a teacher it has become clear to me that the four Gospels contained in the New Testament are an endless supply of wisdom containing more depth and richness than can be plumbed in a single lifetime. Nonetheless, as I have alluded to before, working with these texts now for nearly 19 years, more than 16 as an ordained person, I have come to see five themes (i.e., sutras) appear over and again. In them is the core wisdom of Jesus and they inform how I read the Gospels.

We will dedicate a section of three chapters to each of these sutras/themes in order to explore how they express themselves in the Gospels as well as how we might understand them from a post-modern context. The five themes are:

1. All there is is now: The past is a memory and the future is a fantasy.
2. You are adored by the Divine, and there is nothing you can do to change it.
3. Your relationship with God is about your relationship with others.
4. Morality is about relationships, not rules.
5. The Kingdom of God is at hand.

All there is is now: The past is a memory and the future is a fantasy.

There seems to be a basic human temptation to live in the memories of the past or the anticipation of the future. The difficult reality for our brains and bodies, however, is that they cannot tell the difference and so emotionally we become captive to those memories or anticipations. Jesus regularly calls us to be in the present and to live with what is.

You are adored by the Divine, and there is nothing you can do to change it.

Despite what much of later Christian theology may teach and the popular images of the Christian God as a wrathful father figure bent on the destruction of humanity save for Jesus, Jesus' own message was quite different. Repeatedly throughout the Gospels Jesus proclaims the love of God to those whom the religious establishment deemed outside divine love and redefined what justice in relation to sin looks like.

Your relationship with God is about your relationship with others.

Quintessentially, Jesus articulates this theme with the summary of the law ("You shall love the Lord your God with all your heart, with all your soul, with all your mind, and with all your strength. The second is this: Love your neighbor as yourself. There is no commandment greater than these." - Mark 12:29-31). Love of God is inextricably connected to love of neighbor and vice versa.

Morality is about relationships, not rules.

Jesus breaks custom regarding cleanliness on a number of occasions in order to be in relation to those who are deemed outsiders. His passion and compassion for the poor, the sick, and the outcast become a foundation of his ministry. But these actions are not done as charity and they are not done simply to flout religious customs. Rather they are the embodiment of Jesus' relational understanding of reality and of one's reality in connection to the Divine.

The Kingdom of God is at hand.

In all four Gospels Jesus is recorded as having proclaimed the kingdom of God, and more specifically that the kingdom of God is at hand. Contrary to popular images of heaven, Jesus' image is more shaped by the prophetic tradition out of which he came. This tradition articulated a vision of humanity that rejects domination systems regardless of how they are justified, and substitutes for them a human community where justice and economy are marked by equity (i.e., the needs of all are met by all). His proclamation that this Kingdom is "at hand" is not simply a vision for the future but an invitation into a lived reality that is already present, if only in its potential.

PART II:
ALL THERE IS IS NOW

CHAPTER 6:
THE BURDEN OF BEING SELF-CONSCIOUS –
LIVING WITH MORTALITY

To say that we are self-conscious beings is so obvious as to be a truism. But what do we mean when we say that we are self-conscious? Is it merely that we are conscious of ourselves and the world around us? Or is it that we, by our very nature, have an ability to reflect upon our own existence? In either case, self-consciousness sets us apart from the vast majority of animate life on this planet and has for millennia. When speaking of *Homo sapiens* it is, more than any other, the trait that distinguishes us from the rest of animate life on Earth.

SELF-CONSCIOUSNESS: A GIFT AND A BURDEN

Bishop John Shelby Spong, in his book *Jesus for the Non-Religious*, is monumental in helping us to see the burden that comes with self-consciousness. Most animate life exhibits consciousness of one sort or another, but self-consciousness seems to be limited to humans and a small number of other animals.

Most of us know what it means to be conscious. Put simply consciousness is active awareness of one's surroundings. It is the ability to pick up data from the world and interpret that data in a way that informs a reaction (e.g., the deer who bolts at the snap of a twig, or a driver stepping on the accelerator when the light turns green). Put in the simplest terms, consciousness is the ability to recognize change. We see consciousness all over the place not only in other human beings, but also in our pets; the insects in our gardens; birds on a wire; animals in a zoo; and pretty much anything that walks, flies, or swims. We recognize consciousness in other life forms because we ourselves are conscious and see reflected back our own reality.

But what about self-consciousness? This is more than simply being aware of the world around us and how it changes. It is being able to imagine ourselves in context with that world and to recognize the change within us. It is the ability to see how things were, how they are now, and then to imaginatively project how they might be in the future. With self-consciousness comes the recognition of time and the recognition that just as something outside of myself comes into being, exists, and then ceases to exist, so too will I follow that pattern.

Whether or not any animals other than humanity exhibit self-consciousness is a matter open to quite a bit of debate. But there is no question that at some point in our evolutionary development, humanity became self-aware. And that awareness, all by itself, was a game changer.

It is self-consciousness that allows for us to develop beyond inherited behavior. With self-consciousness, technology becomes something that is carried forward through a model of education, because memory of the past is valued as an adaptation to change. Also, self-consciousness allowed and allows for us to imagine the same internal reality in one another. This led to the evolutionary development of empathy and sympathy, which in turn allowed small packs of hunters to develop into more and more complex social systems (i.e., clan, tribe, village, town, city, state, nation).

But it is also with that development that we became aware of our mortality (i.e., that we will inevitably die one day). And that presented and still presents a significant crisis on multiple levels. Death is an absurdity. Why is it that the wonderful and wondrous mystery of any one person is going to cease to exist? How is the economy of nature served by such a reality? Where is the justice in a natural system that allows for the destruction of other human beings whom we have come to know and without whom we are diminished?

Ancient people asked other questions in the midst of their conscious self-awareness that we ask as well. Why is there disease? Why did it rain today and not yesterday? For what purpose do earthquakes exist? From where does wisdom come? Why am I (and by extension all humans) self-aware? Where did I come from? Where am I going? Does my consciousness cease when my body dies? Etc., etc., etc.

With the advent of the scientific method and the sciences, humanity in the modern era has more and more turned to science to answer many of these questions. But for millennia humanity turned to a different source.

THE PRACTICE OF RELIGION: SELF-CONSCIOUS COPING IN THE FACE OF THE UNKNOWN

What is religion? It is a worthy question to ask. According to *Webster's Dictionary*, religion is "the service and worship of God or the supernatural" or "a personal set or institutionalized system of religious attitudes, beliefs, and practices."[7] But, frankly, this only scratches the surface. Religion was, and for some today still exclusively is, an attempt to make sense of the experience of reality. It is an attempt to take all the data available and organize it into a coherent method that allows one to cope with the burdens of consciousness and self-consciousness. This is true even when one is not fully cognizant of that motivation.

If we stop and imagine our ancient ancestors it is not hard to see them contemplating this awareness we call self-consciousness and wondering from where it came. It is also not hard to imagine how isolating a feeling it created in them, since it still has the ability to create that sense of isolation in us.[8] It is also not hard to understand, even if we don't agree, how they recognized patterns in nature and determined that there must be a like (albeit grander) consciousness behind all things.

Out of that realization (some might call it "projection") religion then took on a variety of forms. In some cultures divinity was understood to exist in multiple gods, each responsible for a different aspect of creation (i.e., polytheism). In others the Divinity was actually in and through all things and expressed itself differently in different forms (i.e., animism). And, rarely, as in the case of the faith of ancient Israel, divinity was expressed in a single deity who transcends all created order and functions as its creator and animator (monotheism).

Regardless, in each and every case the attempt in the practice of religion was to appease the Divine for the purpose of aid and comfort in this life. Often the question of life after death was not even in the equation of ordinary worship. Instead the practice of religion was, as I stated earlier, an attempt to make sense of and gain some control over the environment in which one lived. In most cases the Divine was approached in the same manner as anyone or anything with power would be approached, with deference and the offering of gifts. Coping mechanisms that had developed within the human community, including systems of domination, were simply projected onto the realm of the Divine.

Within a Jewish context, by the time of Jesus, this had developed into the elaborate temple complex and its system of ritual sacrifice. The offering of animals to the Divine and sharing of the meat between the fire of the altar and the worshipper were seen as an act of communion (i.e., meal sharing) with the Divine, which then established righteousness (i.e., a right and favorable relationship with the Divine). Doing such behaviors then allowed one to feel more secure in one's life knowing that God had been satisfied and would be favorable towards you. In other words, if one made sacrifice then one's crops would not fail, one's sheep would not be ravaged by wolves, one's spouse would conceive and bear a son, etc.

THE SOULS OF THE RIGHTEOUS ARE IN THE HANDS OF GOD

The book of Wisdom says "But the souls of the righteous are in the hand of God, and no torment will ever touch them" (Wisdom 3:1). In addition to the day-to-day coping strategy of religion there is also present in it an overt attempt to deal with the question of mortality. Throughout human history different religions have expressed different answers to this question. What may be surprising is that the popular religious notions of heaven that are espoused by today's traditional Evangelicals and Catholics would have been alien to many people in the ancient world, including many Jews. There were, in fact, three ways of understanding the meaning of life and death in Israel at the time of Jesus.

The first idea, which some scholars would argue is the most ancient, is espoused by the Sadducees (the wealthy elite of ancient Palestine) who argue that there is no afterlife and that life on this Earth is a gift from God to be cherished while it is to be had.

The second idea, which was espoused by some of the Pharisees and the overwhelming majority of the underclasses, was the idea of the resurrection of the dead, which ultimately informs the Christian community and the story of Jesus. This position argues that after a righteous person has died they will one day be raised from the dead into a transformed body that will never die again and will experience life as paradise.

The third idea that floated around in the midst of the other two was heavily informed by Platonic philosophy and accepted the notion of an immortal soul. In this idea the body ceases to function and decays, but the consciousness, which animates that body, continues to exist in the presence of the Divine. This model appealed most to the intellectual elite because it allowed them to imagine their intellectual prowess continuing unabated for eternity.[9]

What is of interest, in terms of Jewish practice at the time of Jesus, is that all three systems resolved the question of the meaning of life on the pattern of ritual observance. In other words, religion practiced as a means of making sense out of day-to-day life would result in meaning making out of the question of life and death.

JESUS AND THE BURDEN OF SELF-CONSCIOUSNESS

As mentioned in chapter 4, the Torah was not seen as an ideal to which persons were meant to strive, but rather a practical tool to be applied to the reality of one's life. In this regard, Jesus comes out of a rabbinical tradition that assumes that one of the key goals of religious practice is to make sense out of day-to-day living and to live that life in harmony with God and humanity.

While much effort has been made to spiritualize the teachings of Jesus, frequently Jesus tried to bring meaning to day-to-day living. He often spoke in terms that were commonplace for his time. And his parables almost always dealt in themes that would have been easily accessible to every strata of society. Here are a few examples:

> "Do not store up for yourselves treasures on Earth where moth and rust consume and where thieves break in and steal; but store up for yourselves treasures in heaven, where neither moth nor rust consumes and where thieves do not break in and steal. For where your treasure is, there your heart will be also." (Matthew 6:19-21)

> "The kingdom of heaven is like a mustard seed that someone took and sowed in his field; it is the smallest of all the seeds, but when it has grown it is the greatest of shrubs and becomes a tree, so that the birds of the air come and make nests in its branches." (Matthew 13:31-32)

"Pay attention to what you hear; the measure you give will be the measure you get, and still more will be given you." (Mark 4:24)

"The earth produces of itself, first the stalk, then the head, then the full grain in the head. But when the grain is ripe, at once he goes in with his sickle, because the harvest has come." (Mark 4:28)

"There is nothing outside a person that by going in can defile, but the things that come out are what defile." (Mark 7:15)

"No good tree bears bad fruit, nor again does a bad tree bear good fruit; for each tree is known by its own fruit." (Luke 6:43-44a)

"To what should I compare the kingdom of God? It is like yeast that a woman took and mixed in with three measures of flour until all of it was leavened." (Luke13:20-21)

But in the midst of this, Jesus is asked on more than one occasion, "What must I do to inherit eternal life?" To each questioner he gives a different answer.

Here is the reply to the rich man in the Gospel of Mark:

As he was setting out on a journey, a man ran up and knelt before him, and asked him, "Good Teacher, what must I do to inherit eternal life?" Jesus said to him, "Why do you call me good? No one is good but God alone. You know the commandments: 'You shall not murder; You shall not commit adultery; You shall not steal; You shall not bear false witness; You shall not defraud; Honor your father and mother.'" He said to him, "Teacher, I have kept all these since my youth." Jesus, looking at him, loved him and said, "You lack one thing; go, sell what you own, and give the money to the poor, and you will have treasure in heaven;

then come, follow me." When he heard this, he was shocked and went away grieving, for he had many possessions. (Mark 10:17-22)[10]

In the Gospel of Matthew, Jesus replies to a lawyer in this way:

Just then a lawyer stood up to test Jesus. "Teacher," he said, "what must I do to inherit eternal life?" He said to him, "What is written in the law? What do you read there?" He answered, "You shall love the Lord your God with all your heart, and with all your soul, and with all your strength, and with all your mind; and your neighbor as yourself." And he said to him, "You have given the right answer; do this, and you will live." (Matthew 10:25-28)

In both cases, Jesus seems less concerned with the afterlife than with how this life is lived. He clearly is trying to shift the existential angst of his questioners away from the question of their own mortality to that of a more ordinary type, namely how one lives this life. This makes clear that Jesus' own answer to the question of life and death is rooted in the life we are living.

But this does not mean he precludes the existence of an afterlife either. Listen to this parable he gives in regards to an issue of social justice:

"There was a rich man who was dressed in purple and fine linen and who feasted sumptuously every day. And at his gate lay a poor man named Lazarus, covered with sores, who longed to satisfy his hunger with what fell from the rich man's table; even the dogs would come and lick his sores. The poor man died and was carried away by the angels to be with Abraham. The rich man also died and was buried. In Hades, where he was being tormented, he looked up and saw Abraham far away with Lazarus by his side. He called out, 'Father Abraham, have mercy on me, and send Lazarus to dip the tip of his finger in water and cool my tongue; for I am in agony in these flames.' But Abraham said, 'Child, remember that during your lifetime you received your good things, and Lazarus in like manner evil things; but now he is comforted here, and you are in agony. Besides all this, between you and us a great chasm has been fixed, so that those who might want to pass from here to you cannot do so, and no one can cross from there to us.' He said, 'Then, father, I beg you to send him to my father's house—for I have five brothers—that he may warn them, so that they will not also come into this place of torment.' Abraham replied, 'They have Moses and the prophets; they should listen to them.' He said, 'No, father Abraham; but if someone goes to them from the dead, they will repent.' He said to him, 'If they do not listen to Moses and the prophets, neither will they be convinced even if someone rises from the dead.'" (Luke 16:19-31)

Now while this parable has many layers of meaning woven into it, what seems to be clear is that Jesus is intentionally ambiguous about what happens after we die. When one examines the Gospels one can find examples of him advocating for a resurrection understanding and on other occasions arguing for the idea of the eternal soul dwelling with God in paradise. Either way, however, he is never far from the idea that this life, the one we are in now, is of prime importance and that whatever meaning there is to be made comes not through ritual gesture, but by how we treat our fellow human beings. This is a theme to which we will return in chapters 13 and 14.

CHAPTER 7:
THE PAST IS A MEMORY AND THE FUTURE IS A FANTASY

While the ability to remember events from the past, as well as the ability to anticipate the future, is a great boon to humanity, a question still remains. Why are we so obsessed with the past and the future? If you stop to think about it, most people on any given day are conscious of the present very little. Most of us spend more time either reminiscing or anticipating. In fact, we do it so much that we accept it as normal behavior and we usually treat our memories and our anticipations as if they are as real as what is happening in the present moment. This has as much to do with biology as it does with psychology or spirituality.

MEMORY, FANTASY, AND THE HUMAN MIND

In the field of mind-body studies there is a realm of scientific research called "psychobiology." This is not some "new age" discipline, but a serious and rigorous field of scientific research, which covers a wide range of both mental and physical conditions. It is most commonly known as "behavioral neuroscience" and has produced no fewer than 17 Nobel laureates in the variety of specialties that fall within this field.

What research in this field has indicated is that memory and fantasy are far more powerful in the effect on our brain and bodies than most of us ever imagined. In fact, when a memory or fantasy is vivid enough, our bodies cannot distinguish the memory/fantasy from reality.

The clearest examples of this dynamic are shown in the mental disorders of abuse survivors and combat veterans. Many of these individuals suffer from post-traumatic stress disorder (PTSD), a condition in which they cannot separate the reality of the present from the powerful feelings (both mental and physical) that the memories of past trauma create. And because of this, both groups suffer significant difficulties, often not only socially but medically.

But this principle isn't just true in the case of severe trauma. Studies have shown that none of us are immune to the power of memory or fantasy.[11] In fact, simply watching a particularly well-acted film or play can cause a similar response in the body to having actually been placed in the situation being dramatized. We have recognized this effect for centuries and even have a word for it: catharsis.[12]

So, whether positive or negative, memory of the past and anticipation of the future are powerful motivators for us, often because they do not resolve as quickly as any moment in the present. In fact, when we find that we cannot let go of our memories or fantasies we might well become stuck in a place in time, fixated (perhaps addicted) to the emotional content welling up inside of us in response.

GETTING REAL ABOUT WHAT IS REAL

So a real trap of our ability to remember the past and anticipate the future is becoming confused about what is real and what is memory or fantasy. And that is no small statement. With the power that memories and anticipation can have on us and our bodies it is very easy for a memory to function in the present as if it is the present reality, or for anticipation to equally impact us as if the event we are anticipating is already occurring.

How many of us have found this to be the case? How many of us have spent hours and hours worrying about something that is coming up, or spent moments in sheer agony over what we think is going to happen? I have done just this on more occasions than I care to recall, but one example from my adolescence brings the dilemma into sharp focus.

When I was in the ninth grade I was given the opportunity to work in the office at the junior high school I attended. The facilities were several decades old by the time of my attendance and the telephone system was a relic of the 1950s. Each day a student or member of the staff would have to sit at an operator's manual switchboard and direct all incoming and outgoing calls. Among all the office tasks that a student could be asked to do, to be invited to work the switchboard was considered an honor. Needless to say, when invited to be a phone operator for the school, I immediately accepted.

I went through the training and prepared for my first morning doing the job (which by the way only lasted for an hour, the length of one school period). I would love to tell you that it was a glorious experience, but that was not the case. Instead I became extremely confused and made so many mistakes that an adult had to take over and rescue me. I was ashamed and embarrassed. Worse, my confidence was shot and I was convinced that I would be permanently removed.

To my shock I was invited the next day to sit back down in the same chair and try again. This time I made it through the hour without any major difficulties. In the days and weeks ahead I settled into what appeared to be a relaxed routine.

What no one knew was that each morning I would go through horrific bouts of bowel pain and anxiety because of a double whammy I placed on myself. Quite literally, I became addicted to the memory of my "failure," and by doing so became equally addicted to the anticipation of failure in the day's work ahead. Each day I would reach the end of the hour and realized that there was really nothing to worry about, but the next morning the cycle would recur.

I look back on that time now and feel a great deal of sorrow and compassion for the young man who was so trapped by his own fears and anxieties. I am equally aware of just how much time, energy, and joy was squandered on a fantasy that had no basis in reality.

After having done years of pastoral care, it is clear that stories like these are common and the problem of confusing one's anticipations with reality has most likely been a problem for human beings since the first person became self-aware. The greatest tragedy is that it all too often feels like a trap that is inescapable. But, just as the absurdity of it is apparent to us in this context it has also been apparent to others, most especially Jesus. In fact, one could argue that one of the central tenets of Jesus' understanding of reality was that all there is is now.

While he appreciated the heritage out of which he came, and he equally had a clear vision of humanity for the future (and as well the grisly future to which his own ministry was leading), he did not obsess on the future (or for that matter the past). Rather, again and again throughout the Gospels we see Jesus responding to what presents itself in the present moment and calling on his disciples to not live in anticipation of the new kingdom or in the memory of what was.

Jesus' own words from the Gospel of Matthew best sum up his pattern in regard to past, present, and future:

> "Therefore I tell you, do not worry about your life, what you will eat or what you will drink, or about your body, what

you will wear. Is not life more than food, and the body more than clothing? Look at the birds of the air; they neither sow nor reap nor gather into barns, and yet your heavenly Father feeds them. Are you not of more value than they? And can any of you by worrying add a single hour to your span of life? And why do you worry about clothing? Consider the lilies of the field, how they grow; they neither toil nor spin, yet I tell you, even Solomon in all his glory was not clothed like one of these. But if God so clothes the grass of the field, which is alive today and tomorrow is thrown into the oven, will he not much more clothe you— you of little faith? Therefore do not worry, saying, 'What will we eat?' or 'What will we drink?' or 'What we wear?' For it is the Gentiles who strive for all these things; and indeed your heavenly Father knows that you need all these things. But strive first for the kingdom of God and his righteousness, and all these things will be given to you as well. So do not worry about tomorrow, for tomorrow will bring worries of its own. Today's trouble is enough for today." (Matthew 6:25-34)

It is from this frame that Jesus himself lived and it is out of this frame we can derive a vision of what being in the now looks like.

CHAPTER 8:
TODAY - THE GIFT OF ETERNITY

When the past and the future are recognized for what they are—cognitive constructions—all that is left is the present. But that begs a question, doesn't it? What is left, if now is all there is? As we have already explored, we rely so heavily on ideas about the past and future that, for many of us, the idea of only having the present is a great cloud of unknowing. It is alien territory if we do not spend any real time in the present, and yet it's not that we haven't ever been there. Children often live in the present with little thought to past or future. In fact, if we reckon back to our childhood we might just begin to get an inkling of what life in the present could look like. We also can find something about life in the present from the shape of the life of Jesus and a few things he had to say on the matter. By doing so, we may just discover that the present is not a moment that comes from the future and immediately is relegated to the past, but rather something far more amazing.

LIVING IN THE NOW: FREEDOM FROM ANXIETY

Have you ever noticed that young children, when they are not abused, neglected, or traumatized, are quite literally care free? They seem incapable of worry and do not have an anxious cell in their little bodies. We often attribute this to their age, but I have come to question that presumption. Perhaps the quality we see in them has more to do with their ability simply to be in the now.

Jesus was quite aware of the anxiety produced by remembrance or anticipation. He commends his disciples on many occasions to free themselves of their concern by not living in the past or future. Here are just a few examples where he explicitly speaks about anticipatory anxiety:

> "So do not worry about tomorrow, for tomorrow will bring worries of its own. Today's trouble is enough for today." (Matthew 6:34)

> "When they hand you over, do not worry about how you are to speak or what you are to say; for what you are to say will be given to you at that time;" (Matthew 10:19)

> "When they bring you to trial and hand you over, do not worry beforehand about what you are to say; but say whatever is given you at that time, for it is not you who speak, but the Holy Spirit." (Mark 13:11)

> "When they bring you before the synagogues, the rulers, and the authorities, do not worry about how you are to defend yourselves or what you are to say; for the Holy Spirit will teach you at that very hour what you ought to say." (Luke 12:11-12)

> "And can any of you by worrying add a single hour to your span of life? If then you are not able to do so small a thing as that, why do you worry about the rest?" (Luke 12:25-26)

Another area where he speaks on this matter is one that requires a little bit of contextual understanding to make it explicit. Many people are aware of the beatitudes of Jesus (Matthew 5:1-12 or Luke 6:20-26), which occur within his Sermon on the Mount. But, if you are like me, I grew up hearing those iconic words of blessing and woe more as moral statements than as statements about the reality of life in the now. This comes from understanding the word "blessed" to mean, "favored" or "sanctified." But, the word used in the Greek manuscript is *markarios*, which is more aptly translated "happy" or "fortunate." And the word for woe in Greek, *ouai*, is actually an exclamation of pain and anger and might be more aptly expressed as a groan or the use of profanity. For our purposes, perhaps the best way to express it would be to adopt the language of Eugene Peterson's paraphrase of the Bible, *The Message: The Bible in Contemporary Language*, and translate ouai as "trouble."

For those who are unfamiliar with the text I present a paraphrase of the version found in the Gospel of Matthew with the word "fortunate" substituted for "blessed" and the phrase "trouble" substituted for the word "woe."

> Then he looked up at his disciples and said: "Fortunate are you who are poor, for yours is the kingdom of God. Fortunate are you who are hungry now, for you will be filled. Fortunate are you who weep now, for you will laugh. Fortunate are you when people hate you, and when they exclude you, revile you, and defame you on account of the Son of Man. Rejoice in that day and leap for joy, for surely your reward is great in heaven; for that is what their ancestors did to the prophets. But it's trouble if you are rich, for you have received your consolation. It's trouble if you are full now, for you will be hungry. It's trouble if you are laughing now, for you will mourn and weep. It's trouble for you when all speak well of you, for that is what their ancestors did to the false prophets."

Jesus is describing the transient nature of reality and the impermanence of things by laying out a dichotomy of fortunes and misfortunes that are, by all accounts, paradoxical. In other words, he is saying consider yourself fortunate if you find yourself at the bottom because there's only one way to go from there, and equally saying that it is troubles ahead if you are riding high because there's really only one way to go from there as well. In all of this is in an implicit appeal to stay present. To live for and with what is and not live for what was or what will be.

THE FULLNESS OF TIME: THE ETERNAL NOW

In the Gospels there is a Greek word that roughly translates as "time." It occurs repeatedly, but its meaning is often lost to us moderns because in classical Greek there were two words for time: *chronos* and *kairos*. Chronos is the kind of time we are familiar with. It is the passage of seconds, minutes, hours, days, weeks, months, and years. It ticks by second by second and we mark the changes in the world around us and in ourselves by it. It is a convenient and important method for managing change and organizing our lives.

Kairos, on the other hand, is not about linear time. It is a word with a rich layer of meanings. In classical Greek it often means an opportune time and/or place, or the right time to say the right thing. In the form of Greek in the New Testament (Koine Greek) it carries the additional meaning of a moment in which the purpose of the Divine is fulfilled, or a time in which the Divine breaks through chronological time and is fully present to experience. Often translated as the "fullness of time" or the "time has come," this understanding is used a number of times in the New Testament to describe both the nature of being in the presence of Jesus and the nature of a life in faith. Jesus himself referred to time in this way in both the Gospel of Mark (1:14-15) and the Gospel of John (2:4 and 17:1).[13]

A quintessential example of time from a kairos perspective is the story of Jesus' transfiguration on the mount:

> Six days later, Jesus took with him Peter and James and John, and led them up a high mountain apart, by themselves. And he was transfigured before them, and his clothes became dazzling white, such as no one on earth could bleach them. And there appeared to them Elijah with Moses, who were talking with Jesus. Then Peter said to Jesus, "Rabbi, it is good for us to be here; let us make three dwellings, one for you, one for Moses, and one for Elijah."

He did not know what to say, for they were terrified. Then a cloud overshadowed them, and from the cloud there came a voice, "This is my Son, the Beloved; listen to him!" Suddenly when they looked around, they saw no one with them any more, but only Jesus. (Mark 9:2-8)

In this story we have a clear example of a mystical experience of the in breaking of the Divine in which the normal sense of time and space slip away. The author of this text did not intend for us to take the story literally and uses a number of literary techniques to clue us into the mystical nature of the experience.

First there is the appearance of Jesus in dazzling white. Such an image evokes the Hebrew notion of the glory of God (Hebrew *shekinah*) that radiates a brilliant white light. In the presence of Jesus the fullness of God is being seen, not as a literal light but as a metaphorical brilliance, as the Divine is recognized in him. Further the presence of Moses and Elijah are to ground this experience in the tradition out of which the Jesus' friends and followers are shaped. But most importantly, the whole scene is quickly "overshadowed" by a cloud. Clouds are ancient symbols of mystery that indicate that the story being told is an attempt to convey that which is beyond language and understanding. It is the primary clue that the rules of time and space, empiricism and rationality have slipped away because the experience is outstripping them. And while Peter tries to reground the experience back in the norms of chronological time and space (i.e., staying and building) there is a resistance to such movement and the story takes on a timeless quality in which we are not sure how long it lasted: a minute, an hour, a day?

Such is the nature of time from a kairos perspective. The idea of kairos invites us to experience time in a different way. It is an essential part to all mystical traditions (e.g., Jewish Kabbalah, Christian Mysticism, Zen Buddhism, etc.). It is not, however, a rejection of chronological time, but rather an invitation into a fuller reality. It is, in short, an invitation to eternity.

LIVING IN THE NOW: AN INVITATION TO ETERNITY

Going back to the idea of what life was like when we were small children, did you ever notice how long summer seemed? Or how it seemed an eternity until Christmas? Or how long one day could last?

One of the complaints I hear regularly in my role as a provider of spiritual care is how short time is. How there is never enough time. How life would be so much better if only the person in front of me could find some time for himself or herself.

Responsibilities aside, why is it that we seem to have more time than we know what to do with as children, but seem to be in a drought of time as adults? I don't think it is really about time management as much as it is about where we live. Again, are we living in the past or future, or are we living in the now?

When we give ourselves permission to set aside our anxieties and expectations, when we choose to live in the present rather than be captive to memory or fantasy, an amazing thing happens: Time opens up. Some describe this experience as a slowing down of time, and others as an unwinding of time, but they all point to the same experience.

When we consciously move to the now our sense of time expands and we suddenly find ourselves with a wealth of time that future/past living does not afford. And, because we no longer allow ourselves to be informed by the anxieties created by future/past living many, if not most, of the compulsions that devour our time evaporate.

If you have never had this experience, I invite you to take a moment right now. Upon completion of this paragraph, set the book down. Close your eyes. Take several deep slow breaths and as you are doing so consciously let go of the anxieties and assumptions that are currently holding you captive. Recognize in that moment that all there is is you and your breath. Everything else is a mental construct. All there is is now. Then open your eyes and staying in that place, be still for a minute. When you think a minute has passed look at your watch.

Did you do it? If not, stop and please do the exercise before you continue.

All right. What did you experience? Were you surprised by the experience? What I experienced in that exercise the first time I did it, and what many who I have directed have experienced is that when they rested for a minute and then looked at their watch they came to recognize that only a fraction of a minute had passed (e.g., 20 seconds, 30 seconds, 45 seconds). For a few, more than a minute had passed, but even they expressed surprise because they, more often than not, felt like more time had passed than had actually occurred.

This is the power of now. It is something that was at the core of Jesus' life and an integral part of his pattern. He had the uncanny ability to remain present in any given situation. And while there is no explicit teaching on this dimension of the now it is clear that he treasured the quiet and the openness of such living. It was an integral part of his life to go away for quiet and retreat. In fact, it was in the quiet and retreat of being away with three of his companions that the mystery of his transfiguration is told (Matthew 17:1-8, Mark 9:2-8, Luke 9:28-36). One possible way of looking at that event is to imagine that, in the quiet openness of simply being in the now with Jesus, eternity and the Divine became explicit for those gathered.

PART III:
YOU ARE ADORED BY THE DIVINE AND THERE IS NOTHING YOU CAN DO TO CHANGE IT

CHAPTER 9:
SEPARATION FROM GOD AS AN EXPLANATION OF DEATH

In this chapter we take a step away from the scriptures to do a bit of religious anthropology and philosophy. This will set up our discussion about the radical nature of one of Jesus' themes: You are adored by the Divine.

The basic presumption of both traditional Judaism and traditional Christianity, as religious systems, is that mortality (e.g., death of the body) is a sign of brokenness in the Universe. This presumption can be found in countless texts, including texts of both the Hebrew scriptures (e.g., the Old Testament) and the Christian scriptures (e.g., the New Testament). In fact, many ancient cultures and, in general, humans going back to the Neanderthals have struggled to make sense of death.[14] But this begs the question as to why.

MADE IN THE IMAGE OF GOD?

All of the Abrahamic faiths (Judaism, Christianity, and Islam) affirm that humanity is "made in the image of God."[15] But what exactly does that mean?

There have been many interpretations of the phrase "made in the image of God" and like texts in the Bible, some agree and some disagree. A great deal of them don't ever ask the underlying question of why someone would presume to even ask the question of one's relationship to the Divine. Instead they take that as a forgone conclusion and then use the idea to argue for some particular theological or philosophical position in terms of the nature of humanity or to justify some particular approach to issues of social order or the practice of religion.

Underneath these arguments, though, a quiet voice whispers for attention. It calls out to anyone who is still enough to listen, asking why would an ancient person presume that humanity is made in the image of God?[16]

We actually don't have to go to academic sources to imagine what would cause such an idea to arise. All we need do is look to our own experience, and utilizing the second naiveté argued for in chapter 2, allow our imagination to inform our experience.

If we stop and think about it, the gift and burden of self-consciousness we explored earlier allows us to imagine eternity. It allows us to form images in our minds that stretch endlessly backward and forward. We are capable of imagining a time before this Universe existed and a time when this Universe, as we now understand it, will cease to exist. And while our dominant myths have moved from the realm of religion into the realm of science, it is still nonetheless an imaginative process.

Is it much of a stretch, then, to imagine ourselves as being made for eternity if we can imagine eternity? Even today our principal goal in medicine is to extend human life. Both religious and secular writers imagine ways in which humanity might one day be virtually or entirely immortal. Most Americans, even if they do not describe themselves as religious, affirm their belief in the immortality of the soul and the existence of an afterlife.[17] When I reflect on this reality in my own mind I see that my tendency to accept the idea of life after death is driven less by the fear of death itself than by the absurdity of non-existence.

I believe it is this then that informs the notion of being made in the image of God. It is, if you will, a projection of our experience onto a being for which the experience of eternity is an ongoing reality and not just a mental projection. It is a mental construct for a belief, based on the idea that since we can imagine being outside of time and can imagine eternity, there therefore must be a being that is eternal and not bound by time or space.

Whether we agree in the anthropomorphism of this theistic understanding is not relevant to our point. It simply outlines how one might understand "made in the image of God" and the way the ancient mind of humanity embraced such an idea as an explanation of why we might be able to imagine eternity, but not live in it.

EVICTION FROM PARADISE: MORTALITY AS A SIGN OF OUR ESTRANGEMENT FROM THE DIVINE

We now turn exclusively to Judaism and Christianity to look at how the question of human origin and mortality is resolved. While other ancient cultures like the Greeks and the Egyptians had different foci for their sense of an afterlife and their theology, most of Western culture (which includes you and me) has been shaped by these religious traditions in one way or another.

And so, we come to the story of Creation found in Genesis, in which there is described a time when humanity fully reflects the image of God and is, therefore, immortal. This represents humanity in an idyllic state. As Dietrich Bonhoeffer articulates in *Creation and Fall: A Theological Exposition of Genesis 1-3* the point of the two creation stories in the first chapter of Genesis is not so much to describe a reality that existed before this one as it is to describe and explain why reality was the way it was for the author of the Genesis story. In other words, the story of the fall of humanity in Genesis is an explanation for why humanity has these "divine" qualities and yet is bound by suffering, pain, and death.

The second story of Creation describes a humanity that is innocent, carefree, but diligent and engaged with both the Divine and the world around him/her. When we do not corrupt the story with Platonic idealism, Eden is a place of delight, but not a place of self-indulgence or indifference. It is clear that humanity has a role to play in the created order, but that the duality of work and leisure does not exist. The story has the Divine establish a limit for humanity (do not eat the fruit of the tree of the knowledge of good and evil) and then proceeds through an externalized struggle with temptation to describe what would be for any of us a recognizable condition. As expected, humanity fails to resist temptation and the result is the growth of knowledge. It is this growth of knowledge that then robs humanity of its innocence and an estrangement from the Divine occurs. The eviction from paradise comes not so much as a punishment, but rather as the organic consequence of humanity's behavior (e.g., trying to return to the garden is, quite literally, like trying to return to a state of consciousness that no longer exists). It is at this point that all the dualities of life become a reality for humanity (i.e., pain/pleasure, knowledge/ignorance, life/death, etc.). It is important, however, to note that the estrangement from the Divine is not a creation of the Divine, but a human creation. In the story of Creation, the Divine is seeking humanity and humanity hides. In the end the Divine, rather than allowing the knowledge to destroy humanity, sends humanity into the world. The author(s) of Genesis believe that the human condition is not a product of the Divine, but a product of humanity.

This then establishes the sense of the brokenness of humanity. It is not a moral judgment as much as it is an explanation of the experience. It is recognition of the broken state of the human condition and an explanation for human mortality.

LATER THEOLOGICAL DEVELOPMENTS

While one can argue that there is little or no moralism in the story of Creation and fall, this cannot be said for the Bible as a whole or for the development of religion, specifically in Christianity.

In the intervening millennia following the development of the first five books of the Hebrew scriptures and a number of historical developments (specifically the Alexandrian empire and the rise of ancient Hellenism), the understanding of the state of humanity and its relationship to the Divine became increasingly moralistic and devolved into the scheme more recognizable today.

By the time of Jesus, while the steadfast love and faithfulness of God was still taught and affirmed, equally it was understood that God was displeased with human sin (error of action or thought) and justly angry with humanity. The solution offered was obedience to the law and temple sacrifice. Through these "gestures" humanity was offered a means of reestablishing right relationship with God (e.g., righteousness). Nevertheless, beneath it all was an implicit assumption that the Divine was an angry deity in need of appeasement.

Subsequently, with the influence of Hellenistic philosophy, writers such as Augustine of Hippo, Anselm of Canterbury, and Thomas Aquinas take the notion of divine wrath and human sin to a new level by coming to understand the problem of estrangement from God being not simply something we've done, but part of the nature of who we are.

Such late imperial and medieval theology led to the understanding that the death of Jesus was a blood sacrifice to pay a sin debt. Sacrificial theology had always seen blood as both a literal and symbolic metaphor for the life energy of any living creature. In the sacrifice of animals in the temple, while humanity ate the cooked flesh of the animal, the blood was reserved for God. With God consuming the life energy and the people consuming the flesh, a meal was shared with God and communion with the Divine was accomplished. This was not seen as an act of atonement, but rather a means of maintaining some level of intimacy with the Divine.

In these later theologies, the "debt" of sin is understood to be a life debt with its origins in the sin of Adam and Eve, which cannot be fulfilled by any one person since it is greater than any one life. Jesus, by offering himself for crucifixion becomes the atoning blood offering that, because he is both human and divine, fulfills the life debt owed by humanity.

The problem, however, is that if we accept this explanation of the death of Jesus of Nazareth, then what we have is nothing less than an image of the Divine as an abusive parent who subjects his child to suffering and death in order to pay a "debt" which is owed him. Further, it taints the meal established by Jesus on the evening before his death with this ideology and deprives it of any real sense of intimacy with the Divine.

Needless to say, this is a theology that is increasingly difficult to accept for many modern people who see this as nothing more than a model of divine abuse and a justification for the abuses of persons and systems within organized religion.

CHAPTER 10:
GOD AS FATHER

If we are to take the witness of scripture not as history but as the portrayal of the shape of a life lived, then what we have in Jesus is something very different from his contemporaries. There was, in fact, no shortage of miracle workers and several other figures contemporary with Jesus who were acclaimed as messiah.[18] But, while the Gospels record miraculous acts and signs, and Jesus is quoted as having said, "I have not come to bring peace, but a sword" (Matthew 10:34), Jesus was, by and large, neither a miracle worker nor a militaristic messiah. No, rather than either of these he was first a religious reformer and, second, a social reformer. His pattern and proclamation has more in common with the prophetic tradition of Israel than it does with supernaturalism or the violent independence movements of the zealots.[19]

No, this person who was called Jesus of Nazareth was quite unique among the voices of his day and offered a radically different vision. This is not to say he wasn't critical of the social order of his day and was a fan of the domination system of Rome. But, in the end his message focused on non-violent resistance and his vision for humanity was based on a fundamental belief that the estrangement with God that most people accepted as truth was, in fact, part of the domination system that needed to be dismantled.

A central theme that undermined the notion of estrangement and the image of the Divine as an angry deity was his use of the word *abba* when addressing the Divine.

FATHER: GOD AS PARENT

A number of authors have popularized Jesus' use of the word "abba" as a form of address for God. While it is true that Jesus regularly addressed God as father, the Aramaic word for God, "abba" is found in the Greek manuscripts of the Gospels only three times. Nonetheless, it remains true that on numerous occasions Jesus can be found encouraging his disciples to think of and address the Divine as father.

What is most striking, however, is that the use of the word "abba," or anything akin to it, to address the Divine would have been seen by most of Jesus' contemporaries as irreverent and inappropriate. While the popular urban myth that "abba" means "daddy" has been disproved, it nonetheless bespeaks of a very different relationship to God than was the norm in first-century Palestine.

While ideas of God as loving and faithful were affirmed in first-century Judaism, a dominant theme of God as transcendent and totally other took prominence over any kind of language of intimacy. This becomes expressed ultimately in the unspeakable nature of God's name. With such a pervasive sense of the otherness of God and the dominance of punitive images of the Divine, the idea of framing one's relationship with the Divine in the familiar and intimate language of parent and child, at best would have seemed ludicrous and, at worst, outright blasphemous.

When we take into account that the word "father" is used no fewer than 34 times in the New Testament to refer to the Divine and the record of Jesus using the word "abba" in at least three circumstances (possibly more), then we are left with an image of the Divine very different than what we assume to be the tradition of Christianity.

If God is, in fact, our heavenly "father," then the notion of an angry, vengeful deity is rejected. Moreover, it becomes abundantly clear that for Jesus, the central image of God is one of deep intimacy and trust. It is the relationship described between the first humans and the Divine. It is a relationship that is built on an understanding of the Divine that had become alien in Jesus' context and alien in our own.

Jesus takes this idea of God as parent in the deepest sense to a visceral level in one of his teachings:

> "Is there anyone among you who, if your child asks for bread, will give a stone? Or if the child asks for a fish, will give a snake? If you then, who are evil, know how to give good gifts to your children, how much more will your Father in heaven give good things to those who ask him!" (Matthew 7:9-11)

> "Is there anyone among you who, if your child asks for a fish, will give a snake instead of a fish? Or if the child asks for an egg, will give a scorpion? If you then, who are evil, know how to give good gifts to your children, how much more will the heavenly Father give the Holy Spirit to those who ask him!" (Luke 11:11-13)

It would be easy, because of the pattern of assumptions, to focus in on the statements about the evilness of those to whom Jesus is speaking. But Jesus does not presume that those to whom he speaks are evil. This is a clear indication of the effective use of hyperbole as a means of making a point.

The average person who heard Jesus would have probably felt they did a decent job of parenting and would not have labeled themselves as evil in regard to this function. Jesus is then asking the listener/reader to imagine the God they have been taught to think of and compare that to their own parenting. What parent would behave so dreadfully to a child? If in our finitude we can do better than this, why would we not accept and recognize that the Divine is equally up to the task and would be just as, if not more, compassionate and caring?

So the appeal to God as father serves as a rejection of a vengeful deity and an invitation—a köan if you will—into the mystery and wonder of a God who is devoted to humanity with a level of love and caring that can best be expressed in a parenting frame.

JESUS' OWN INTIMATE RELATIONSHIP WITH GOD

The cynic may respond to referring to the Divine as a parent as simply "pie in the sky" theology, which when tested fails the test. Perhaps this seems true for some, but Jesus' understanding of the intimate and caring relationship of God was something to which he clung to the very end. When looking at the three occasions when the word "abba" is used it becomes clear that, for Jesus, this was not simply a good idea, but a conviction of heart, mind, and spirit that informed his own spirituality and the ways in which he taught others about the Divine.

In the Gospel of Mark we have a direct instance of Jesus using the term "abba" in relation to God on the evening of his betrayal:

They went to a place called Gethsemane; and he said to his disciples, "Sit here while I pray." He took with him Peter and James and John, and began to be distressed and agitated. And he said to them, "I am deeply grieved, even to death; remain here, and keep awake." And going a little farther, he threw himself on the ground and prayed that, if it were possible, the hour might pass from him. He said, "Abba, Father, for you all things are possible; remove this cup from me; yet, not what I want, but what you want." (Mark 14:32-36)[20]

Further, in the Gospel of Luke, Jesus at his own crucifixion is quoted as saying "Father, forgive them; for they do not know what they are doing" (Luke 23:34). And, his last words from the cross are, "Father, into your hands I commend my spirit." (Luke 23:46a).

Such usage leaves us with no choice but to see Jesus' persistent use of "father" and "abba" for the Divine as a rejection of images of God that are aloof and impersonal. As we move forward, we will explore the implications of this understanding of the Divine in terms of how we understand our relationship to the Divine and how we develop an ethic for living.

To reiterate, we are left with a God who is not an aloof and impersonal being, nor is the God of Jesus a vengeful and angry one either. Instead we are asked to imagine and embrace a relationship with the Divine that is deeply intimate, marked by compassion, and filled with the caring, nurture, and protection one finds with a parent.

SOME IMPLICATIONS OF SUCH A RADICAL SHIFT

If we stop to ponder the implications of such a shift in thinking it is quite striking. This shift for which Jesus argues and which informs his own approach to living is nothing less than a revolution and a major developmental shift in human consciousness.

If, prior to this understanding, the dominant and principal theme of religion was divine appeasement, then much of one's energy was taken up trying to make God (or the gods) happy so that one's life was manageable and bearable. It was a presumption of hostility in the world, both natural and supernatural. And further, with the theological development of the notion that we were to blame for it all and doomed to repeat the mistake forever there wasn't much hope for any real sense of meaning and purpose to one's life, save for survival.

But what happens when all of that changes around and the Divine becomes a loving, supportive, involved, and invested source in one's life? What does one then do with the energy once devoted to compensating for a failed nature and the appeasement of an angry deity? And for that matter, when everyone you know is invested in and committed to the pattern of appeasement, the belief in the depravity of humanity, and a religious system committed to the service of an angry deity, how hard is it to accept such a radical notion that we are, in fact, adored by the Divine?

It is this sociological reality, namely the inability to accept the idea of a loving deity, which has undermined Jesus' own teaching on the matter. For reasons that are perfectly understandable the message was just "too good to be true." And for most of the history of Christianity, humanity has worked very hard to develop a religious system that embraces the rhetoric of Jesus' teaching without the substantive content.

How else do we comprehend a religious system dedicated to the concept that God is love, but is committed to marginalizing anyone who does not conform to orthodoxy of thought, or a specific pattern of living? Furthermore, if not because of social patterning and an unwillingness to accept divine love, compassion, and care, how do we understand the regular swelling up of pietistic practices that are, in fact, forms of ritual, psychological, and often physical abuse or self-abuse?

Needless to say, however, these patterns are as old as humanity and were present in Jesus' own context. To our benefit, the Gospels capture Jesus' own answer to the dilemma posed by such patterns. It is to this answer that we turn in the next chapter.

CHAPTER 11:
LOVE ONE ANOTHER
AS I HAVE LOVED YOU

So given that there is an overwhelming precedent in Western human thinking to explain mortality as an expression of estrangement from the Divine, and an appreciation of, but inherent resistance to, the idea of an intimate and loving Divinity, how then does one overcome the obstacle, in order to not simply think that God loves us, but experience it as a lived truth? This is the anthropological and theological dilemma that has gripped Christianity for two millennia and, at least in terms of anthropology, has gripped much of Western culture (either explicitly or implicitly) for much of the same time.

Within his own context, an inherently Hellenized Jewish context, Jesus too had to deal with this dilemma. His answer was to emphasize a pattern from his own religious tradition that established an ethic for living. But before we examine this ethic, we must first look at an assumption implicit in Jesus' teaching.

KNOWING DIVINE LOVE

How does one know the love of the Divine? Most people who answer that question without any further framing would point to the evidence of benefit in their life (e.g., I am successful, I am wealthy, I am healthy, I have a job that is meaningful, etc.). In fact, for much of the history of humanity the means of determining whether the Divine is expressing love or anger has been directly tied to the notion of blessing and curses, or rewards and punishments. Whether looking at the plays of classical Greece or the covenants of the Hebrew scriptures, there is no shortage of sources portraying the anger or love of a deity through the nature and quality of the life of a human subject. In Jesus' own day, illness was understood to be the consequence of sin, a curse from God. In the relative near past of Puritan America, it was commonplace to believe that material success was a sign of God's blessing (read "love"). Academics, like 19th-century sociologist Max Weber, have shown that in many contexts this assumption of divine blessing being tied to material success motivated people to gain more material success so that they could have the confidence that they were indeed part of God's favored.

But for Jesus, the answer to how one experiences divine love appears to be quite different. When one looks at the pattern of his living and the things he taught it seems clear that, for Jesus, one comes to know the love of God through one's relationships with other people. In fairness this is not an idea unique to Jesus,[21] but it is an idea that is revolutionary in comparison to how most religious systems traditionally treat the question of divine love.

When we look at with whom Jesus ate and drank, with whom he associated, and the various strata of society to which he allowed himself to participate, what we find is a person who is less concerned with appeasing the Divine through ritual purity than someone for whom the Divine is experienced in day-to-day living. We find a man who on a regular basis experiences in his own life an abiding sense of the Divine and the love of the Divine both in and through his relationships with others. But lest we become soppy with a romantic image of love, we must be clear that the idea of love in Jesus own context was not so much a feeling as a norm for behavior.

CHESED: THE LOVE OF GOD

A central idea of the love of God in the Hebrew Scriptures captured in the word *chesed*. In numerous occasions throughout the Hebrew scriptures the nature of God's love is described with the word "chesed" and is traditionally translated as "mercy" or "kindness." To put it mildly, chesed is a rich word with a depth of meaning that defies any short definition. Simple translations like "mercy" or "kindness" appear because of the Greek Septuagint's use of the Greek word *eleos* as a translation for "chesed." But, when one looks to Hebrew sources and at the variety of ways in which chesed is used, a better (but still limited) translation is "steadfast love and faithfulness."

Chesed, more often than not, stands as an attitude rather than a behavior. It is something that is not only expressed by the Divine, but also by humanity. It is part of a covenant relationship (a relationship of promise and trust). So it is far more than kindness or mercy. In chesed there is steadfastness as one would express in a commitment. There is also conveyed in chesed (principally in the writings of the prophet Jeremiah) a sense of the loving kindness of God, which will not let go of humanity. Again, in this particular context, the notion of faithfulness is at heart. But also in the midst of this is a notion that the justice of the Divine is embodied in the mercy of the Divine. In numerous texts from the prophets it is clear that the attitude of the authors is that Israel is not deserving of the Divine's faithfulness, commitment, kindness, and love. And so, within the word is also a sense of compassion and mercy.

It is no coincidence, then, that Jesus came up with a theology that seeks divine love in a human context rather than a ritual one. A text that apparently informs Jesus' own pattern, as well as that of the writers of the Gospels, is Hosea 6:6: "For I desire steadfast love and not sacrifice, the knowledge of God rather than burnt-offerings." The term "steadfast love" is a translation of chesed. I believe it is an attitude such as this that moves Jesus away from a ritual understanding of one's relationship to the Divine and toward a relational one.

THE SUMMARY OF THE LAW: LOVE OF GOD AND LOVE OF NEIGHBOR

Because of this deep connection between Hosea 6:6 and the notion of chesed, when Jesus is quizzed about the greatest commandments among the Torah he does not simply quote Deuteronomy 6:5 ("Love the Lord your God with all your heart and with all your soul and with all your mind.") He also quotes Leviticus 19:18 ("You shall love your neighbor as yourself."), and says that it is of equal status to the first.

Deuteronomy 6:5 is part of a core text within Jewish tradition. It is an inherent part of daily Jewish ritual. It is part of the daily prayer called the *shema* ("hear, O Israel, the Lord our God the Lord is one"). But it is also a passage that is in no way romanticized or sentimentalized. Love of God, in the context of Deuteronomy 6, was primarily understood more as knowledge than emotion. It was understood as a state of mind rather than a feeling.

On the other hand, love of neighbor as spoken of in Leviticus 19:18 has always been intrinsically linked to how one behaves towards another. Initially "neighbor" was understood as countryman, friend, or ally, but over time came to be known more and more generally as acts of justice and compassion to fellow human beings. In fact, the interpretation of Leviticus 19:18, among other passages, as being about chesed is what ultimately informed and created Hasidism within the Jewish tradition. It is this chesed understanding of Leviticus, informed by Hosea 6:6 that Jesus brings to the question of the greatest commandment.

By equating these two passages Jesus is saying, in fact, that one comes to experience the chesed of God through acts of chesed to one another. In other words, one comes to know the love of God (commitment, fidelity, trust, mercy) by means of experiencing these things in the context of human relationships. We will explore this more completely in Chapter 13.

LOVE ONE ANOTHER AS I HAVE LOVED YOU

In the Gospel of John, during Jesus' final conversation with the disciples the night before he dies he tells them, "I give you a new commandment, that you love one another. Just as I have loved you, you also should love one another. By this everyone will know that you are my disciples, if you have love for one another."

The word "disciple" in Greek means, quite literally, "student." But colloquially we can understand what Jesus is saying is that if they love one another as Jesus has loved them then everyone will know that they are living out of the same understanding (i.e., the same worldview) as Jesus. And what is that worldview? Namely that the love of God is known through human relationships and that the primary human relationship they have known to inform that is the one they have had with Jesus.

The Gospels are intended to present to the reader the shape of the life of Jesus, and thereby allow the reader to experience Jesus in a similar manner to the way in which the disciples experienced him. The assumption is that the encouragement of Jesus in this passage applies not only to those who were in the upper room that night two millennia ago, but to us as well.

YOU ARE ADORED BY THE DIVINE AND THERE IS NOTHING YOU CAN DO TO CHANGE IT

Jesus persistently reverts back to the idea of love as a means of understanding our relationship to God and to one another. In this way he goes to the heart of the matter, arguing that the love of God is knowable by how we choose to live our lives. By living an ethic of love (commitment, fidelity, trust, mercy) we open ourselves up to a universe of the same. By offering the chesed of the Divine to others we become open to receiving that chesed in our own lives.

In short, Jesus is committed to the idea that the Divine adores each of us and there is simply nothing we can do to change it. It is a reality whether we are aware of it or not, and that reality compels us to understand our relationship to the Divine and to others in ways different than the religious categories we assume to be exclusive to the Divine. It erases the artificial lines of secular and sacred. It moves us to a place of deep respect and mutuality in which the Divine is present in every person we meet (even our enemies).

The implications of this are huge for how one is to live one's life if consciousness of the Divine and of the Divine's love is desired. It is upon this core theme that the next two themes arise.

PART IV:
YOUR RELATIONSHIP WITH GOD IS ABOUT YOUR RELATIONSHIP WITH OTHERS

CHAPTER 12:
THE PARABLE TRADITION

Jesus' commitment to the love of the Divine, and that this love is knowable through an ethic of interpersonal relationship, has clear implications. For one, it means that metaphysics has significantly less weight in the pursuit of Divine knowledge than we might presume. And while such a conviction does not eliminate the possibility of a metaphysical reality, it does relegate it to a secondary tier. More important, such a conviction places the theme to which we turn in this and the next two chapters in a central location. Namely, if you want to understand your relationship to the Divine, look at your relationship with other human beings.

STORYTELLING AS A MEANS OF UNDERSTANDING ONE'S RELATIONSHIP TO GOD

Jesus' commitment to our relationship to the Divine being expressed in human terms comes through over and again in one of his principal teaching methods, the use of parables (i.e., storytelling). The Gospels record Jesus sharing no fewer than 44 parables[22] with the people he encountered.

Storytelling, as has been shown through modern educational studies, has immense value. Listeners encounter both familiar and new language patterns through story. Both tellers and listeners find a reflection of themselves in stories and factual information is more easily absorbed in the context of story.[23]

Jesus himself appears to have recognized the power and place of story. This is of no great surprise, since the central texts of his own tradition (Torah) were narratives that told the origin stories of his people in relation to the Divine. In fact, story as a way of making meaning was commonplace in the ancient world.

When looking at Jesus' storytelling what we encounter is a variety of methods. Some of his parables are not much more than a sentence, while others are elaborate stories that draw the reader into the narrative. In each case, however, the point is to invite the reader into some deeper understanding of the Divine either directly or indirectly.

Whether he is saying a simple parable like "No one sews a piece of unshrunk cloth on an old cloak, for the patch pulls away from the cloak, and a worse tear is made. Neither is new wine put into old wineskins; otherwise, the skins burst, and the wine is spilled, and the skins are destroyed; but new wine is put into fresh wineskins, and so both are preserved" (Matthew 9:16-17); which serves to critique religious observance. Or, he is telling an elaborate story, like:

> "In a certain city there was a judge who neither feared God nor had respect for people. In that city there was a widow who kept coming to him and saying, 'Grant me justice against my opponent.' For a while he refused; but later he said to himself, 'Though I have no fear of God and no respect for anyone, yet because this widow keeps bothering me, I will grant her justice, so that she may not wear me out by continually coming.' And the Lord said, 'Listen to what the unjust judge says. And will not God grant justice to his chosen ones who cry to him day and

night? Will he delay long in helping them? I tell you, he will quickly grant justice to them.'" (Luke 18:2-8a);

Where he is describing the value of persistence in prayer, he is teaching something about the nature of the Divine and the nature of humanity's relation to the Divine.

I HAVE SPOKEN TO YOU OF EARTHLY THINGS: JESUS' FOCUS ON THE ORDINARY

The most powerful and palpable aspect of Jesus' use of parable is its accessibility. While much of the cultural content that would have been apparent to first-century Palestinians is lost on modern readers, these parables still have a level of accessibility that is startling if one stops to think about it. Why is that?

Again, Jesus' understanding that the Divine is accessible in the ordinary of everyday life appears inherent in Jesus' method when we take a closer look. There isn't a single parable that does not reference something common to the human experience of the people to whom he spoke. And, while Jesus does quote the scriptures on multiple occasions, rarely does he use scripture or anything else recognizably "spiritual" for his teaching about the nature of faith and one's relationship to the Divine.

Here is a quick survey of all the images that can be found in Jesus' parables: new cloth, new wine and wineskins, lamp on a stand, wise and foolish builders, money lending and debt forgiveness, a rich man and opulent living, wise and foolish servants, fig trees, sowing seed and soil conditions, weeds among wheat, mustard seed, yeast, hidden treasure, pearl, fishing nets, cleaning, coins, sheep and shepherding, Samaritans, wedding banquets and banquets in general, rebellious children and a forgiving father, begging and poverty, wealthy indifference, Abraham, wealth management, tenants, vineyards and laborers, widows and judges,

Pharisees and tax collectors, sheep and goats, and angels and heavenly glory.

What is most striking about that list is that the images of Jesus' storytelling do not include anything that would not have been easily imaginable by the people who heard him. Further, there is a conspicuous dearth of God, heaven, biblical images, and the like. In fact, there are only three parables, which directly incorporate such images (Lazarus and the rich man in Luke 16:19-31; the rich fool in Luke 12:15-21; and the separating of the sheep and goats in Matthew 25:31-36).

This is not to say that Jesus is not concerned about the Divine or matters spiritual, but rather to show that his method of conveying such content is primarily through ordinary means and principally through stories that involve a human context.

When we look at the parables that are fully developed stories and not simply one- or two-line sayings, we can see that Jesus is often using a deeply human story and the interpersonal dynamics of that story as a metaphor for the ways in which we connect to the Divine (either directly or through other human beings).

A clear example of this, using a relatively short parable, can be seen when we examine an incident in which Jesus is eating with Pharisees when Jesus forgives a woman of ill repute:

> One of the Pharisees asked Jesus to eat with him, and he went into the Pharisee's house and took his place at the table. And a woman in the city, who was a sinner, having learned that he was eating in the Pharisee's house, brought an alabaster jar of ointment. She stood behind him at his feet, weeping, and began to bathe his feet with her tears and to dry them with her hair. Then she continued kissing his feet and anointing them with the ointment. Now when the Pharisee who had invited him saw it, he said to himself, "If this man were a prophet, he would have known who and

what kind of woman this is who is touching him—that she is a sinner." Jesus spoke up and said to him, "Simon, I have something to say to you." "Teacher," he replied, "speak." "A certain creditor had two debtors; one owed five hundred *denarii,* and the other fifty. When they could not pay, he cancelled the debts for both of them. Now which of them will love him more?" Simon answered, "I suppose the one for whom he cancelled the greater debt." And Jesus said to him, "You have judged rightly." Then turning towards the woman, he said to Simon, "Do you see this woman? I entered your house; you gave me no water for my feet, but she has bathed my feet with her tears and dried them with her hair. You gave me no kiss, but from the time I came in she has not stopped kissing my feet. You did not anoint my head with oil, but she has anointed my feet with ointment. Therefore, I tell you, her sins, which were many, have been forgiven; hence she has shown great love. But the one to whom little is forgiven, loves little." Then he said to her, "Your sins are forgiven." But those who were at the table with him began to say among themselves, "Who is this who even forgives sins?" And he said to the woman, "Your faith has saved you; go in peace" (Luke 7:36-50).

We can see that in this case the temptation on the part of the Pharisees to judge Jesus because of his willingness to be made ritually unclean. But Jesus' response is not to get into an argument over the finer points of the law, or moreover to start quoting the scriptures. Instead, even with those who are quite versed in the religious tradition, he describes a situation that would have been seen as outside the normal realm of religion, a scene that spoke in everyday ordinary terms and described a basic human interaction. When the obvious answer to the question about this situation is given by his critics, Jesus is then free to offer an interpretation for his behavior grounded in something outside the preconceived notions of his religious tradition. Thus, he makes the Divine accessible in a way that was otherwise unavailable.

Some parables are so rich that they convey multiple messages and meanings, so much so that the Gospel writers themselves avoid the temptation of interpreting the story for the reader. One such story comes from the Gospel of Luke. It has been known by several names (i.e., the story of the prodigal son, the parable of the foolish son, the parable of the lost son, the parable of the forgiving father, etc.).

There was a man who had two sons. The younger of them said to his father, "Father, give me the share of the property that will belong to me." So he divided his property between them. A few days later the younger son gathered all he had and travelled to a distant country, and there he squandered his property in dissolute living. When he had spent everything, a severe famine took place throughout that country, and he began to be in need. So he went and hired himself out to one of the citizens of that country, who sent him to his fields to feed the pigs. He would gladly have filled himself with the pods that the pigs were eating; and no one gave him anything. But when he came to himself he said, "How many of my father's hired hands have bread enough and to spare, but here I am dying of hunger! I will get up and go to my father, and I will say to him, 'Father, I have sinned against heaven and before you; I am no longer worthy to be called your son; treat me like one of your hired hands.'" So he set off and went to his father. But while he was still far off, his father saw him and was filled with compassion; he ran and put his arms around him and kissed him. Then the son said to him, "Father, I have sinned against heaven and before you; I am no longer worthy to be called your son." But the father said to his slaves, "Quickly, bring out a robe—the best one—and put it on him; put a ring on his finger and sandals on his feet. And get the fatted calf and kill it, and let us eat and celebrate; for this son of mine was dead and is alive again; he was lost and is found!" And they began to celebrate. Now his elder son was in the field; and when he came and approached the house, he heard music and dancing. He called one of the slaves and asked what was going on. He replied, "Your brother has come, and your father has killed the fatted calf, because he has got him back safe and sound." Then he became angry and refused to go in. His father came out and began to plead with him. But he answered his father, "Listen! For all these years I have been working like a slave for you, and I have never disobeyed your command; yet you have never given me even a young goat so that I might celebrate with my friends. But when this son of yours came back, who has devoured your property with prostitutes, you killed the fatted calf for him!" Then the father said to him, "Son, you are always with me, and all that is mine is yours. But we had to celebrate and rejoice, because this brother of yours was dead and has come to life; he was lost and has been found" (Luke 15:11-32).

Regardless of what one calls this story, its richness points to the poignancy of the human condition and Jesus' undying conviction of the persistent love of the Divine. It shows the love of the Divine and the nature of one's relationship to the Divine being played out not on a heavenly stage, but a very human one. And yet while this is clearly a metaphor for the relationship of humanity to the Divine, like in most of his other parables there is no explicit mention of spirituality or the Divine.

CHAPTER 13:
THE SUMMARY OF THE LAW

While we have touched on the topic of Jesus' summary of the law in response to the question of which of the laws of Torah is the greatest, it is important for us to come back to this topic as it relates to the theme of understanding our relationship to God in terms of our relationship to others. A more thorough examination of the two passages Jesus quotes and likens to one another will help to make even more explicit the degree to which Jesus sees the Divine at work in and through human relationships.

HEAR, O ISRAEL: THE GREATEST COMMANDMENT

When quizzed as to what the greatest commandment is, Jesus is quick to reply, "You shall love the Lord your God with all your heart, and with all your soul, and with all your mind" (Matthew 22:37). But what the casual reader may not realize is that Jesus is truncating a passage from the book of Deuteronomy that has its own rich history and tradition. Deuteronomy 6:4-9 reads:

> Hear, O Israel: The Lord is our God, the Lord alone. You shall love the Lord your God with all your heart, and with all your soul, and with all your might. Keep these words that I am commanding you today in your heart. Recite them

to your children and talk about them when you are at home and when you are away, when you lie down and when you rise. Bind them as a sign on your hand, fix them as an emblem on your forehead, and write them on the doorposts of your house and on your gates.

These sentences of scripture were and are so central to the practice of Judaism that they are traditionally recited twice daily (in the morning and in the evening). They are an act of fidelity to the service of the Holy and traditionally seen as a daily recommitment to the covenant established by Moses.

But the idea of love in this passage does not necessarily convey the understanding that one loves God in any romantically emotional sense. Instead, love is understood to be a state of mind rather than a feeling. It is a statement of ethics. It is the presumption that once one loves God fully then the law is no longer necessary. In other words, to know God is to be in a relationship of commitment and fidelity, a relationship that shapes and patterns one's living. To love God, in this sense, is the ultimate expression of the law.

But there is a deeply radical idea imbedded in this short declaration. The idea that the Divine loves humanity is not all that radical. As we have discussed in an earlier chapter, in many places prior to this passage, the notion of God's steadfast love and faithfulness (i.e., chesed) is affirmed again and again, but this passage implies something far more radical. First, is the radical notion that the chesed of God is something of which humanity is capable, and second is the idea that the Divine desires that this love be returned through the way in which one lives.[24]

LOVE YOUR NEIGHBOR AS YOURSELF

But Jesus, when asked about the greatest commandment does not simply offer the passage from Deuteronomy 6:9, instead he quickly adds the second half of Leviticus 19:18 and says that the two are "alike."

This sentence from the book of Leviticus comes within the context of a whole raft of regulations regarding interpersonal relationships. Each of them outlines ethical behavior in regards to the persons who make up one's community and one's family. There is a presumption in this chapter of Leviticus that the well being of the human community is as dependent upon an attitude of respect and compassion, as is the practice of one's devotion to the Divine.

The Levitical chapter includes provisions for idolatry, food purity, providing welfare for the poor and aliens, theft, ethical business practices, lying, fair wages and employment, fair treatment of those with blindness or deafness, judicial justice, slander, murder for profit, preserving familial ties, respect of one's community members, a multitude of religious restrictions (including issues of sacrifice, diet, witchcraft and body marking), care of the elderly, and fair treatment of aliens.

Moreover, the presence of verse 18, which is lodged in the middle of this list, indicates that this is more than simply a manual for conduct, but is intended to be a psychological and spiritual orientation toward the members of one's community and family. Verse 18 makes it abundantly clear that simply abiding by these rules is not sufficient, but rather these rules are to lay out the cursory boundaries for a mindset that makes the spiritual and material well-being of others as important as our own well-being.

Again, like in Deuteronomy 6, the concept of love here is not a particularly emotional understanding of that word. Instead love is seen as an act of justice or equity of behavior. Love of self is not some form of narcissistic self-devotion as much as it is what we might call a healthy self-esteem. It is understood to embody in the individual the faithfulness and commitment of a community that has entered into covenant with one another and with the Divine.

I DESIRE NOT YOUR SACRIFICES: JESUS AND THE LOVE OF NEIGHBOR AS AN ACT OF LOVING GOD

Simply to look at the two passages explicit in Jesus' reply to the questions of the Pharisees is incomplete, if we are to see how significant human relationship is to his understanding of devotion to the Divine. Instead we must again look to the tradition out of which he came, and more specifically at the prophetic tradition of Israel.

The prophet Hosea puts in the mouth of God, "For I desire steadfast love and not sacrifice, the knowledge of God rather than burnt-offerings" (Hosea 6:6). Like in passages we've examined before, the reference to steadfast love is a reference to chesed.

This passage in Hosea comes directly in the middle of the book and is the declaration of the Divine in response to the lack of faithfulness of Ephraim and Judah. But it is not a lack of ritual behavior, or worship devotion that is the problem within these Jewish lands. No, the issue is the lack of commitment, fidelity, mutuality, justice, mercy, compassion, and communal interdependency that causes the judgment that Hosea speaks on behalf of the Divine. When reading the first five chapters of Hosea the image one derives is of a people who live wholly self-centered materialistic lives that capitalize on the weaknesses of others. It is an environment where the practice of religion has moved from a way of living in community to a pattern of pietistic devotion. It is for this reason the judgment concludes with the quote above from Hosea 6:6, in which chesed (e.g., mercy, kindness, compassion, fidelity, trust, mutuality, etc.), and not ritual gestures, is expressed as the desire of the Divine.

It is my belief that Jesus had this passage in mind when bringing Deuteronomy 6:5 and Leviticus 19:18 together and equating the two. When we look at the context of each passage as we have done, reflect upon the rich meaning of the word chesed, and place them in the context of Hosea 6:6, a complete picture of the relationship between God and other human beings comes into focus.

The implications of this are significant. Unlike sappy sentimentalism (i.e., we have to be nice to one another), or rigorous legalism (i.e., break the law and go to jail), Jesus envisions a sober and engaged pattern of living that opens us to the mystery and wonder that is the other. It is a world in which each human encounter is marked by respect, dignity, mutuality, commitment, and trust. It is an encounter that has as its hallmark a quality of mystery and a respect for the unknown.

When such an encounter occurs, one comes face to face with the mystery of one's own being. One is called into a relationship with self as well as with the other. But this is not the self we presume to know; instead it is a self that is always unknown and yet always willing to reveal itself when we are quiet enough to be attentive. It is a time and space that, while absolutely mundane and commonplace, is also marked in its mystery by the presence of the source of all being. It points beyond itself, drawing us into a sense of the greater reality in which we all participate.

Put simply, when we can fully live into this way of relating with others it is nothing less than a direct encounter with the Divine and exceeds any experience that ritual or prayer can achieve.

CHAPTER 14:
WHO IS MY NEIGHBOR?

Whether explicitly or implicitly, on more than one occasion the question about who is or is not a neighbor comes up in conversation with Jesus. And it comes not just from his opponents, but also from his most intimate followers. Questions about compassion, mercy, and forgiveness all raise questions about just how far Jesus' embodiment of the chesed of God should go.

When we stop to think about it, except in the cases where the questions are posed to create an ensnarement, it is a perfectly reasonable question to ask. In our own time it has become an axiom that we can't do everything and we must first take care of ourselves before we take care of others. We are regularly warned about the dangers of overextending ourselves, "watering down" the impact of our actions, and depleting our resources. But underneath both the concerns raised with Jesus and our own contemporary concerns is a basic desire for survival. And the survival anxiety they felt and we feel is more about anticipation than the reality of now. In this case, as in every case, Jesus presumes that the need presented now outweighs the anticipation of scarcity in the future and calls us to think in much broader terms about the idea of neighbor.

COMPASSION TO THE NEIGHBOR IN BIBLICAL JUDAISM

As we have already explored in the previous chapter, the idea of compassion to neighbor is not new with Jesus. There is within the Hebrew scriptures a long history of expressing care and concern for one's neighbors.

In the earlier texts of the Bible, like the passage from Leviticus 19, the definition of neighbor is someone who quite literally is a part of your community. It is someone with whom you share your life and upon whom your life is, in some way, dependent. There is clear understanding that neighbors do not include those outside of your community (the alienated, the dispossessed, and foreigners). But even here, at least to some degree, provision is made for outsiders. Leviticus 19:33-34 specifically says, "When an alien resides with you in your land, you shall not oppress the alien. The alien who resides with you shall be to you as the citizen among you; you shall love the alien as yourself, for you were aliens in the land of Egypt: I am the Lord your God." Despite this provision, there is a distinction made between a foreigner and someone who is a part of the community, and classical Judaism understood neighbor to be only those who were faithful to the God of Israel.[25]

Nonetheless, there is equally a universalizing tradition within Judaism from the time of the prophets, which can be read to embrace a broader interpretation of neighbor. The book of Isaiah is generally agreed to be actually three books bound together under one name and represents three generations of prophetic writing. Beginning in the second book and continuing into the third is an emphasis that the God of the Israelites is not simply their God, but the one and only God, the God of all history, and the God of all peoples. While a special relationship between the Israelites and God is affirmed, it is clear from this textual tradition that it is understood that all humanity comes under the influence of this one God and that all humanity shall receive the benefit of the Divine.

This is an important development in the spiritual thought of the Jewish tradition because it moves the notion of the Divine out of a simply tribal religion that insures the safety and longevity of a nation-state into a deeper and more transcendent reality. It further allows for passages, like the ones in Leviticus 19:18 and 19:33-34, to be interpreted to mean that love of neighbor extends to all persons and not just those within your community. It is out of this interpretive mix that Jesus' vision arises.

WHO IS MY NEIGHBOR? - THE PARABLE OF THE GOOD SAMARITAN

The parable of the Good Samaritan becomes the primary text, which articulates Jesus' own understanding of what defines an act of love to neighbor.

> Just then a lawyer stood up to test Jesus. "Teacher," he said, "what must I do to inherit eternal life?" He said to him, "What is written in the law? What do you read there?" He answered, "You shall love the Lord your God with all your heart, and with all your soul, and with all your strength, and with all your mind; and your neighbor as yourself." And he said to him, "You have given the right answer; do this, and you will live." But wanting to justify himself, he asked Jesus, "And who is my neighbor?" Jesus replied, "A man was going down from Jerusalem to Jericho, and fell into the hands of robbers, who stripped him, beat him, and went away, leaving him half dead. Now by chance a priest was going down that road; and when he saw him, he passed by on the other side. So likewise a Levite, when he came to the place and saw him, passed by on the other side. But a Samaritan while traveling came near him; and when he saw him, he was moved with pity. He went to him and bandaged his wounds, having poured oil and wine on them. Then he put him on his own animal, brought him to an inn, and took care of him. The next day he took out two denarii,

gave them to the innkeeper, and said, 'Take care of him;
and when I come back, I will repay you whatever more you
spend.' Which of these three, do you think, was a neighbor
to the man who fell into the hands of the robbers?" He said,
"The one who showed him mercy." Jesus said to him, "Go
and do likewise." (Luke 10:25-37)

In this passage Jesus presents again the summary of the law in
response to the question, "What must I do to inherit eternal life?"
This question is not presented by just anyone, but by a "lawyer."
We need to understand that "lawyer" does not, in this context,
mean attorney. Rather, "lawyer" means a person who argues about
Torah. It would be better to understand this person, using today's
language, as a biblical scholar.

And so, in response to Jesus' answer the scholar does not want to
be outdone and wants instead to prove himself no slouch. So he
asks a rhetorical question, expecting the opportunity to debate
Jesus. Instead Jesus tells the story of the Good Samaritan. At the
conclusion of the story, Jesus asks the question as to who did the
will of God. The only appropriate answer was to name the
Samaritan, although the scholar seems not to be able to do it by
name. Why? Because it is in the Samaritan that the chesed of God
and the chesed one expects in a fully actualized humanity is
expressed. The exchange ends with Jesus telling him to go and do
likewise.

This is an important and powerful story for several reasons. First, it
makes explicit that not only is the concept of neighbor not limited
to one's family, tribe, or nation, but also that neighbor is
determined more by one's behavior or need than anything else. In
fact, Jesus never actually answers the scholar's question directly.
Much like an Eastern köan, Jesus leaves the question of who the
neighbor is up to the listener/reader. Instead he describes an
interaction in which the command to love is both ignored and
embodied and calls the listener/reader to reflect on which
behavior best expresses the presence of the Divine.

Who is the neighbor in this parable? Is it the Samaritan or is it the man who is injured on the road? Both interpretations are equally valid. One could argue that the man injured is the neighbor of the Samaritan because his needs and his helplessness are so great. One could equally argue that the Samaritan is the neighbor because of his willingness to empathize with the stranger and engage in a selfless act of compassion. A third equally valid answer would be to say that both understandings are true and that Jesus is more concerned with the behavior than the definition of neighbor.

Regardless, it is clear that by choosing someone who would not have been popularly understood as a neighbor—someone who was, in fact, from a class of people that suffered regular bigotry within contemporary Jewish culture—Jesus is broadening the definition of neighbor to include those people who were outside the community of faith, and who were not adherents of religious custom. The Samaritan, from a modern perspective, might be seen as equivalent to a person of color in a racist environment: easily recognizable and quickly feared and dismissed. But in Jesus' story a neighbor is someone who is colorblind.

In stark contrast, Jesus' description of the adherents to religious tradition and custom, those within the culture of ancient Israel, exhibit none of the compassion, mercy, or commitment that express chesed. Their actions show a meticulous adherence to ritual purity customs, since the victim on the road might be dead and therefore unclean. In each of these characters and their behavior, again we see survival anxiety, and how religious systems can be co-opted into participating in such systems.

The Samaritan, however, "took pity" on the man. This act of mercy is the embodiment of chesed. And his behavior that follows is the fleshing out of his mercy and care. In this story, a neighbor is someone who has compassion for someone in need. But compassion alone is insufficient. The Samaritan also exhibits his chesed in his commitment to the needs of this injured man and his willingness to make a significant investment in his recovery.

Regardless of how you understand who the neighbor is in this passage, the message is clear. Love of neighbor isn't about who is inside or outside of one's community. Love of neighbor is about chesed—about behaving in a way that is compassionate and committed to the needs of others whether or not they are people you know.

LOVE YOUR ENEMIES: BROADENING THE SCOPE EVEN FURTHER

As a part of the Sermon on the Mount in chapter 5 of the Gospel of Matthew, Jesus broadens the idea of who is one's neighbor beyond anything known in the Hebrew scriptures. He says:

> "You have heard that it was said, 'You shall love your neighbor and hate your enemy.' But I say to you, 'Love your enemies and pray for those who persecute you, so that you may be children of your Father in heaven; for he makes his sun rise on the evil and on the good, and sends rain on the righteous and on the unrighteous. For if you love those who love you, what reward do you have? Do not even the tax collectors do the same? And if you greet only your brothers and sisters, what more are you doing than others? Do not even the Gentiles do the same? Be perfect, therefore, as your heavenly Father is perfect.'" (Matthew 5:43-48)

This passage comes at the end of a long line of statements that start with "you have heard that it was said" and ends with "but I say to you." In these passages Jesus is challenging the popular wisdom of his day, as well as several of the entrenched religious attitudes of his culture.

Again, if we stop and think about it, what Jesus says in this passage is just as challenging today as it was two millennia ago. In the wake of countless dictatorships which have maimed, tortured, and murdered and the rise of terrorism in the world who would be interested in forgiving one's enemies? It is certainly not a value expressed in the political arena, nor in popular media. And yet, for Jesus, it is an essential part of the concept of love of neighbor.

The "I say to you" passages which come immediately before this passage lay out what love of one's neighbor looks like and ultimately what love of one's enemy looks like as well. Three specifically bear looking at:

1. You have heard that it was said to those of ancient times, "You shall not murder"; and "whoever murders shall be liable to judgment." But I say to you that if you are angry with a brother or sister, you will be liable to judgment; and if you insult a brother or sister, you will be liable to the council; and if you say, "You fool", you will be liable to the hell of fire. So when you are offering your gift at the altar, if you remember that your brother or sister has something against you, leave your gift there before the altar and go; first be reconciled to your brother or sister, and then come and offer your gift. Come to terms quickly with your accuser while you are on the way to court with him, or your accuser may hand you over to the judge, and the judge to the guard, and you will be thrown into prison. Truly I tell you, you will never get out until you have paid the last penny. (Matthew 5:21-26)

2. Again, you have heard that it was said to those of ancient times, "You shall not swear falsely, but carry out the vows you have made to the Lord." But I say to you, "Do not swear at all, either by heaven, for it is the throne of God, or by the earth, for it is his footstool, or by Jerusalem, for it is the city of the great King. And do not swear by your head, for you cannot make one hair white or black. Let your word be 'Yes, Yes' or 'No, No'; anything more than this comes from the evil one." (Matthew 5:33-37)

3. You have heard that it was said, "An eye for an eye and a tooth for a tooth." But I say to you, "Do not resist an evildoer. But if anyone strikes you on the right cheek, turn the other also; and if anyone wants to sue you and take your coat, give your cloak as well; and if anyone forces you to go one mile, go also the second mile. Give to everyone who begs from you, and do not refuse anyone who wants to borrow from you." (Matthew 5:38-42)

In these passages Jesus again lays out the basic pattern of chesed, which we have encountered repeatedly. He takes extremes and reinterprets them in broad ways that make any act that objectifies the other, or is concerned only with the self, contrary to a life in the Divine.

By asking us to love our enemies he now has extended the idea of love of neighbor to the broadest reaches to include even those who wish us harm. It is a radical concept that is difficult to embrace, but one which marked the early Christian community and was worthy of comment by a number Hellenistic sources.

WHY SUCH A BROAD DEFINITION OF NEIGHBOR?

While there are examples of a teaching such as this in other traditions (even within Judaism at a later point), why would Jesus express such a commitment to the love of all humanity?

It is, I believe, because of his belief in the themes we have already articulated, principally his understanding that we are adored by the Divine and that through us the love of the Divine is expressed.

How else do we know love except through our relationships, and how else do we know the Divine? It seems clear from all that we have explored in the last three chapters, that Jesus understood that what we can truly know from the Divine and about the Divine comes not through speculative religion, but through a specific ethic of living in the context of human relationships. These relationships then make the Divine a living reality in our lives and the lives of others, and open us up to the outpouring of the Divine's love in our life.

With that being the case then the practice of religion, specifically in its ethical and moral dimension takes on a whole new approach that is outside the simple and simplistic indictments of a religious authority. Morality becomes about how one lives in relation to others and not simply about obedience to an arbitrary set of rules.

PART V:
MORALITY IS ABOUT RELATIONSHIPS, NOT RULES

CHAPTER 15:
WHY HAVE RULES?

As the title for this section implies, Jesus' approach to the question of ethics and morality also forms a core theme in the shape of his life and teaching. But this theme does not arise out of a vacuum. Rather, it emerges organically out of the first three themes. Saying that morality is about relationships and not about rules, however, does not imply that Jesus had no regard for rules. To the contrary, numerous scholars (both Jewish and Christian) have pointed out that Jesus clearly was, to an overwhelming degree, adherent to the customs, norms, and mores of Judaism. As the Gospel of Matthew reports, Jesus said, "Do not think that I have come to abolish the law or the prophets; I have come not to abolish but to fulfill. For truly I tell you, until heaven and earth pass away, not one letter, not one stroke of a letter, will pass from the law until all is accomplished" (Matthew 5:17-18). With this in mind and as the title of this chapter expresses, it is better to see Jesus' teaching implicitly raising a more primary question: Why have rules?

Much like in Chapter 9, in this chapter we take a step away from the narratives of the life of Jesus and turn to a broader discussion of why we human beings feel compelled to make rules and how we come to see them as authoritative. This will allow us in subsequent chapters to recognize how Jesus' approach to the question of morality and ethics is radically grounded in human experience and understood, at its best, as an expression of the Divine.

ANXIETY AND THE NEED FOR CERTAINTY

If we stop and recall the discussion we had in Chapter 6 about self-consciousness and the burden that comes with our recognition of our own mortality we can quickly see why societies throughout history have gravitated toward the establishment of rules and the enforcement of laws.

As self-conscious beings we have the ability not only to remember the past, but also to imagine what might happen in the time ahead of us. This perpetually places us at a point between two psychological and existential realities: past and future. And, while an argument can be made that the past has its own burden, for our purposes it is the burden of the future upon which we will focus.

To say, "No one knows what the future will bring," is a truism that almost does not deserve to be mentioned. But, it is this very reality that creates the burden of self-consciousness. There are general truths about the future that we can know with some degree of certainty (e.g., I will need to eat and drink; I will need shelter; I will need clothing; I will need to sleep; I will need a certain amount of social interaction; I will one day die), but the specifics of who, what, where, when, why, and how are a mystery. It is precisely the absence of details, and the uncertainty that it imposes, that creates anxiety in us. Ultimately, the animal survival instinct inexorably turns our psyche to the question of mortality and with that turn comes significant anxiety boiling in our guts.

But as a species, we cannot sustain high levels of anxiety forever. In the end, such strain becomes a burden too great even for the strongest of us. The threat of suffering—or worse, annihilation— drives us to seek out certainty whenever and wherever we might find it. Anecdotally speaking and from my perspective as a helping professional, it strikes me that much of human society is a response to this diffuse anxiety. We create social structures, which include rules, as a response to uncertainty. Specifically, we establish a system of norms and mores with clear rules for behavior (i.e., a system of ethics and morality) as an attempt to create some day-to-day sense of certainty.

Making rules has been a part of the social equation for all of recorded history. It is a common human trait. And while the rules have varied from society to society, again and again human beings have established rules in a variety of ways to minimize our anxiety about the future and to create as much predictability and stability as possible.

In many cases the created rules have simply been unspoken norms within a group. They have been a set of positive behaviors to which everyone subscribes without any thought or discussion. In other cases they have been unspoken mores, by which everyone recognizes a behavior as taboo. But in some cases, when the anxiety is high enough, rules are made explicitly into law and enforced by a governing authority and with the threat of punishment.

As an example, in American culture, when someone enters an elevator, it is expected that he or she will turn around to face the doors. An example of a social norm violation would be to enter the elevator and remain facing the rest of the people. People conform to society by following social norms[26] and by doing so create stability and a sense of predictability. But no one would dare dream of having someone arrested for such behavior. Why? Because the violation of that norm does not sufficiently raise the anxiety about certainty or mortality to warrant such an action. But if that same person were to not simply stand facing the others in the elevator, but were to touch them in an aggressive or sexual way then anxiety would be sufficiently raised and the police would likely be called. At that point any one of us observing such a behavior would not simply call the behavior rude or bizarre, but criminal. It is the threat of such behavior and the fear of its occurrence that inspires the enactment of a law to criminalize it.

One need only look at the laws which a society has enacted to see where the greatest anxiety in that culture is and where human beings, at that time and in that place, have felt most threatened in terms of the predictability of their future and their mortality. Rarely do societies write laws to embrace or codify positive behavior. Even when the language is put in an affirmative tone it is almost always in response to a perceived threat.[27] It is important to remember that laws are always about anxiety and are almost always about restricting behavior rather than encouraging it.[28]

THE PROBLEM OF AUTHORITY

But this raises another fundamental question. What happens when someone in a society refuses to accept the rules by which that culture operates? Another way of saying this is that the problem of authority always arises when there is a diversity of opinion and varying levels of anxiety around a stable future and the threat to survival. From what or to what authority does one appeal for such rules?[29]

This is, in fact, why societies write laws. When there is agreement about the rules there is no need for laws, because there is no need to enforce laws and no need to appeal to a higher authority for those laws. Laws come as a direct response to anxiety in the face of behavior that is seen as a threat to stability or survivability.

Authority can be ascribed to the Divine (usually interpreted by an individual or a clergy caste), to an ideal (although this usually requires someone or a group of people to interpret the ideal), to an individual (e.g., a monarch, a tyrant, a dictator), to a small or elite group of people (e.g., nobility, aristocracy, or oligarchy), or from the population in general (e.g., social contract, or democracy). Regardless of which system is chosen, one of these will become the authority to which the culture will appeal when there is a sense of threat.

The point is that whether one is in a theocracy (i.e., ruled by a religious system), a domination system (i.e., tyranny or oligarchy) or in a collective society (e.g., social contract or democracy), for the system to work there needs to be a collective agreement by a majority of people that those who govern have authority and that the rules enacted represent a shared set of values that create a sense of stability that stave off anxiety. Without this the alternative is chaos and anarchy.

COLLECTIVE AGREEMENT: RELATIONSHIPS TRUMP RULES

Put simply, rules only serve their purpose when there is collective agreement to abide by those rules and to grant authority to someone to enforce those rules. Societies collapse when there is a sufficient lack of agreement on what rules are authoritative and who has the authority to enforce them.

This is a significant point, because this means that ultimately the question of morality does not come from thin air, but rather comes out of a relational process that takes place with human beings interacting with one another in a social context. Ultimately rules are secondary to relationships. It is the relationships that form between people that provide the foundation out of which rules arise.

Even when the authority to which one appeals is one's own ancestors (e.g., biblical authority), there is still the need to agree collectively that such an authority is valid and that the norms, mores, and laws which are derived from that authority are collectively binding. The number of groups, just within Christianity, which hold differing views on biblical interpretation, style of worship, church governance, and ethical/moral teaching is staggering, and points to the issue of authority when determining the rules.

NATURAL LAW: THE PHILOSOPHY OF RELIGION

At this point, a logical question arises, however. Aren't there some things that, unless you are a psychopath, everyone agrees are appropriate or inappropriate behavior? Aren't there some things that are so common that they might be described as simply organically true? This question points to an idea that arises within the field of the philosophy of religion and is called "natural law."

Many people subscribe to a natural law approach without ever using the term. Most of us, at some point in our life lived out of a theory of natural law. It is most common for children to do so. We see right and wrong as obvious and natural. We do not question the rules by which we live, but understand them as self-evident arising out of the very fabric of our lives.

Within philosophical discipline, however, there are, in fact, two different ways of understanding the concept of natural law. The first argues that certain moral propositions have their own objective truth that transcend any particular place or time and can objectively be known because they contain their own truth.[30] The second understanding argues that standards of morality are derived from the nature of the world and the nature of human beings.[31] In both cases, however, the problem still exists as to where the authority for interpreting such matters arises. In both cases there is a presumption about a shared reality, an accord if you will, that informs how we interpret the sense data we receive. Regardless of what you call that authority (reason, nature, etc.), there still is the thorny issue of how you define what you experience. This inevitably leads to an appeal to an interpretive authority and moves us once again towards a relational and collective understanding of what constitutes morality.

Having said all of this, the point of this chapter is not to undermine the important place that rules have within human experience, but to be explicit about their purpose and from where they come. Just as Jesus affirmed the importance of the Torah in Jewish life, we too need to recognize the importance of the variety of rules that validly exist within human society and to honor their value and place in our lives. But, there is also a place to critique the rules by which we live and, at times, to violate them and reject them.

It is with this understanding that we can then begin to look at the pattern of Jesus' own ethical and moral teaching and see that his understanding of morality was shaped by his understanding of the inherently relational quality of rules and the inherently relational quality of our life in the Divine.

CHAPTER 16:
BREAKING THE RULES FOR THE SAKE OF RELATIONSHIPS

Even when there is general agreement among a group of people to abide by certain rules, that doesn't mean those rules are positive or constructive. As we outlined in the last chapter, rules are ultimately about the reduction of anxiety and not necessarily about matters of justice, equity, compassion, mercy, faithfulness, or kindness (or whatever ideal to which we wish to point). In short, just because someone feels less anxious from the enforcement of a rule, doesn't mean that chesed, in any of its variety of expressions, is being encouraged or protected. It falls much into the same category as the modern American dilemma that the ideal of liberty in law is not the protection of liberty in reality. Throughout the United States' history there have been numerous laws couched in the language of liberty that have, except for the privileged few, guaranteed its antithesis. It is this very tension that shapes the ethical and moral behavior of Jesus and of the behaviors he encourages in others.

BY WHOSE AUTHORITY?

We don't need to look very hard at the Gospels to see that Jesus is regularly accused of flouting the norms, mores, and laws (both Jewish and Roman) of his own society. The Gospel of Luke records the following encounter Jesus had with those who represented religious authority in his own social context:

> One day, as he was teaching the people in the temple and telling the good news, the chief priests and the scribes came with the elders and said to him, "Tell us, by what authority are you doing these things? Who is it who gave you this authority?" He answered them, "I will also ask you a question, and you tell me: Did the baptism of John come from heaven, or was it of human origin?" They discussed it with one another, saying, "If we say, 'From heaven,' he will say, 'Why did you not believe him?' But if we say, 'Of human origin,' all the people will stone us; for they are convinced that John was a prophet." So they answered that they did not know where it came from. Then Jesus said to them, "Neither will I tell you by what authority I am doing these things." (Luke 20:1-8)

Even within their own context, the Jewish authorities of Judea recognized the tension between their authority and that of Jesus. Further, their internal dialogue, as reported in this story, shows recognition that authority is, at least in part, derived from a relational environment. But, this in no way stops them from challenging Jesus about his authority openly. Why? Because of Jesus' open critique of the way in which the religious tradition is being interpreted by those authorities. Such a critique and the popularity of it with the crowds create a threat for those in power. Insecurity is born out of the unpredictability of both Jesus and the crowds. The fear of loss of power, loss of livelihood, and even a possible threat to life (from the Roman authority) is embedded in such a situation. It is a very human and understandable reaction

Jesus experiences from those who question his authority. The question of authority is always central when someone begins to behave in ways contrary or threatening to the rules established by those in power.

Often, within a secular context, those in power will appeal to the imagery and ideals of the society or to some icon of those ideals (e.g., freedom, liberty, the Constitution, etc.). In religious contexts, however, those in power turn to the Divine and claim the rules they represent are divinely mandated. For Jesus it was a "double whammy" as the temple authorities represented, in many ways, both religious and civil culture in ancient Judea.

But the power system that the temple authorities represented was, in fact, a domination system. It was a social system common to the ancient world, in which power and wealth rested in the hands of a tiny minority and the vast majority of people lived at their mercy. Whether one looks to Rome, or the monarchies of the ancient Near East, again and again what one finds is a system of norm, more, and law that was designed to keep stable the economic and power structures that benefited the wealthy and powerful minorities in those societies.

This meant that the overwhelming majority of wealth at the time of Jesus was vested in the monarchy and the temple. What was left was taxed heavily and shipped off to Rome to support the wealth and comfort of the capital city and its imperial apparatus. The rhetoric, regardless of context, was about peace and prosperity. But few in such a culture actually experienced it.

In fact, the morality code which had become commonplace was one based on conquest and domination. Whether it was the slave trade of conquered nations, the power of wealth to dominate the poor, or the bankruptcy of farmers and the alienation of populations from their lands, the model was clear: He who wins gets to control, gets to decide, gets to impose order, and if a few people die in the process, so be it. Better that than war, poverty, chaos, and death.

16: BREAKING THE RULES FOR THE SAKE OF RELATIONSHIPS

Kings, emperors, and the aristocracy rule for the "benefit" of society and it is the obligation of everyone else to obey. Whether that model was being waged by the imperial legions of Rome or by the temple authorities in their models of manipulation and control, a critical voice would not/could not be tolerated. The moral vision of salvation through victory and domination was the only vision that would be tolerated.

The difficulty, however, was that the vision of the Hebrew scriptures was, as we have seen, quite different from that of a domination system. In the scriptures one finds a moral vision rooted in concepts of equality, fair and equal distribution of wealth, a justice system based on equality before the law, and laws based on chesed (i.e., commitment, fidelity, trust, and mercy).

Whether one looks at the articulation of Torah in Exodus, Leviticus and Deuteronomy or at the various expressions of morality expressed in prophets such as Isaiah, the message comes through over and again that morality is about creating a just and equitable society and that it is the Divine's intention for all humanity to live to its fullest potential and to not be predatory upon one another.

Moreover, the blessings of the Divine are secured when the community chooses to live in this manner. Or, to be more precise, the Divine is made manifest in the context of human community (e.g., family, neighborhood, class, assembly, town, city, state, nation) when we live with one another in a way such that our relationships are marked by commitment, conscientiousness, trust, and compassion. When we live with one another in a way in which chesed is practiced, then a society forms that is marked by legal justice, economic justice, and social justice. But in order for that to happen, love of neighbor (i.e., chesed) must be a normative part of how human beings behave toward one another.

This is significant, because we could easily see the above as a material argument for how society functions and not make any connection whatsoever to the Divine. But for Jesus, this image of

132

society and how we interact was inherently tied to the Divine. In fact, it was at the core of his understanding of how we know and understand the Divine. To live in community in this way is to encounter the Divine in a direct and tangible way!

And so it is out of this understanding that Jesus speaks and acts with authority. It is an authority that does not rely simply on rhetorical ability or external authority, but arises out his radical authenticity and his commitment to a model of living that is based not on domination but on love of neighbor.

LOVING YOUR NEIGHBOR: A MORAL VISION

So then, what does love of neighbor look like? How does it get lived out? Jesus had a very different answer than that of his contemporaries who supported the domination models of the day.

For those who subscribed to such domination models, love of neighbor was confined to how one behaved toward those who maintained an absolute adherence to the purity laws of Judaism, and to those who practiced the remainder of Torah without blame. Much like the material blessing principles of New England Puritans of the 17th century, common wisdom in Jesus' time was that if someone was poor or ill, then that was a sign that they had failed to maintain the law. There were those who challenged this notion and an intellectual "dodge" was created by using a text from Exodus,[32] that said if someone was righteous but still in a state of suffering, then one of that person's ancestors must have committed a sin, and the righteous person suffering was doing so for the sake of their ancestor's sin.[33] This ideology could be applied to physical ailments, but also to financial, social, or political calamity as well. In this way the religious system, despite all that it had to say in critique of the domination system, became complicit with it.

Jesus, however, rejected such notions and saw the love of neighbor as being intrinsically connected with the love of the Divine. Does this mean that he condoned immoral behavior, or discounted it for the sake of being kind to those on the outside? Put simply, no. Never once does he excuse behaviors that are in violation of the core of Torah teaching.[34]

For Jesus the notion of chesed, the idea that we are adored by the Divine, and the fundamental dignity of all human life are essential. For him, any behavior that objectifies another person is inherently immoral. A clear example of this can be seen in his parable of the Pharisee and the tax collector:

> He also told this parable to some who trusted in themselves that they were righteous and regarded others with contempt: "Two men went up to the temple to pray, one a Pharisee and the other a tax collector. The Pharisee, standing by himself, was praying thus, 'God, I thank you that I am not like other people: thieves, rogues, adulterers, or even like this tax collector. I fast twice a week; I give a tenth of all my income.' But the tax collector, standing far off, would not even look up to heaven, but was beating his breast and saying, 'God, be merciful to me, a sinner!' I tell you, this man went down to his home justified rather than the other; for all who exalt themselves will be humbled, but all who humble themselves will be exalted." (Luke 18:9-14)

The central character in this story is not the tax collector, but the Pharisee, and the central axiom is not the Pharisee's self-aggrandizement, but his belittling comparison of the tax collector to himself. It is the radical objectification of the mystery of another human being that is the central fault of the Pharisee and the genuine humility of the tax collector that stand juxtaposed.

In the wake of the models of modern psychology, we are quick to assume that the tax collector is simply being self-deprecating and to uncritically assume that Jesus is endorsing such behavior. But we should not be so quick to project our understandings on a text such as this. It is equally possible to understand that what we have here is a view into how two different people approach the question of humanity and the Divine. One approaches with an attitude of arrogance and authority (i.e., presumes to know all there is to know), while the other approaches with an attitude of humility and awe (i.e., engages reality as mystery). Which of us has not been struck by our smallness and felt a similar state of humility (even if not marked by penitential language) when contemplating the vastness of reality?

And so, it is in the frame of non-objectification that Jesus again and again engages those who are on the outside of society. It is with such a frame of reference that he is known to be "a glutton and a drunkard, a friend of tax collectors and sinners" (Matthew 11:19). Whether it is the woman caught in adultery (John 8:1-11), the Samaritan woman at the well (John 4:1-42), tax collectors (Matthew 9:9-13 and Luke 19:1-10), sinful women (Luke 7:36-50), a woman with a menstrual hemorrhage (Matthew 9:20-22; Mark 5:25-34; Luke 8:43-47), the possessed (Mark 5:1-20), or lepers (Mark 1:40-45 and Luke 17:11-19) it is out of an unwillingness to objectify that we again and again see Jesus engaging those who otherwise would have been shunned or ignored.

The only way to understand such a behavior is to recognize that he saw the love of neighbor as being something that trumped those laws that kept people separate from one another. Further, he openly rejected the use of any law, norm, more, or code of conduct as a means of objectifying another human being. To do so is nothing less than an objectification of the Divine and arrogance verging on hubris.

And so, for Jesus to violate the norms of his culture for the sake of relationship was, in fact, the moral thing to do. By doing so he affirmed the deep morality of chesed and the more authentic ethics of his religious tradition. While these violations would ultimately be one of the central causes of his criminalization and execution, it was an inevitable behavior for Jesus. To have denied the dignity of another would have been to deny the Divine.

CHAPTER 17:
THE SABBATH WAS CREATED FOR HUMANS, NOT HUMANS FOR THE SABBATH

When looking at Jesus' non-conformist behaviors in regard to popular understandings of Torah obedience, the quintessential example of his behavior's intentional unmasking of the use of the Divine as a guise for something else comes in his perpetual violation of the Sabbath.

SABBATH: YOU SHALL CONSECRATE A DAY OF REST

Sabbath is a central and early concept in the development of Torah. It is found in the poetic rendering of the Creation in Chapter 1 of Genesis and the narrative rendering of the story of Creation in Chapter 2. In both cases, the texts tell us that even the Divine takes rest after having created the world and all that is in it.

This is a recognition on the part of ancient peoples of the deep benefit and value of rest. It is a part of the concept of chesed, in that it appreciates the need to admit the needs of others and to cease activity. There is a variety of ways of understanding the development of such a law. One might argue that the prohibition to work was an attempt to secure the health and safety of the community by insuring that exhaustion and the hazards that come with it were prevented. Another might argue that the rule of rest was an attempt to insure religious observance in the community. A third option might be that the Sabbath law was in reaction to harm that had already beset the community from a lack of self-care. It may well be that it becomes a central tenet of Judaism because of the Israelites' collective memory of slavery. Regardless, even today, the need for rest and rejuvenation is understood to be of vital importance and a core benefit to humanity.

Regardless of how or why, the sanctity of rest is ultimately codified in the recitation of the Ten Commandments in Exodus:

> Remember the Sabbath day, and keep it holy. Six days you shall labor and do all your work. But the seventh day is a Sabbath to the Lord your God; you shall not do any work— you, your son or your daughter, your male or female slave, your livestock, or the alien resident in your towns. For in six days the Lord made heaven and earth, the sea, and all that is in them, but rested the seventh day; therefore the Lord blessed the Sabbath day and consecrated it. (Exodus 20:8-11)

However, by the time of Jesus, out of this short declaration a list of 39 forbidden Sabbath activities[35] had developed. To do them to any degree was seen as an act of disrespect to the Divine and a violation of one's relationship with God. Further, out of this list of 39 generalized activities came a host of interpretive texts that made clear how one was to adhere to this restriction. There were, in fact, so many interpretations that the 39 activities came to be understood as 39 categories of activity. Most of such interpretation in Jesus' own time was oral and passed on through an oral tradition.

Needless to say, the idea of instituting a day of rest for all people is commendable and is something from which our work-driven culture today would benefit. But, to codify such a norm into a set of laws, which has 39 categories, which subsequently has dozens of interpretations in each category, is to create a morass of confusion that makes the observance of rest a chore in itself.[36] It is this understanding of Sabbath that Jesus challenges by willfully disregarding it.

VIOLATING THE SABBATH: THE "WORK" OF JESUS

The question that immediately arises for us in light of this historic reality is, who benefits from such a confused and confusing system of control? A system such as this is designed for one purpose: to keep people under strict control. The more complex a law becomes the harder it is to keep it. As long as the population continues to accept that the law is valid, then there is ample cause to impose greater and greater restrictions (read "punishments") on those who violate the law. A psychological system of fear and domination can quickly develop that keeps large numbers of people under control.

Such a system also allows for those who are making the rules to understand themselves as being of a higher status or superior to others. For example, if we are wealthy and privileged, then rules prohibiting basic tasks on a "day of rest" are of no real concern, as we will have servants who can do such things for us. We are then prone to see such restrictions as reasonable and necessary for all. But, if we are poor and struggling, then we may well have to violate those rules in order simply to survive. If we are loyal to the system that established these rules, it instills within us a sense of unworthiness—or worse, depravity—that undermines our ability to critique the injustice in the system. And with that we have a system in which those who are privileged remain privileged, and those who are not remain marginalized.

17: THE SABBATH WAS CREATED FOR HUMANS, NOT HUMANS FOR THE SABBATH

It is in this environment, informed by his understanding of the sacredness of all human relationships that Jesus acts. On multiple occasions Jesus engages in debate over Sabbath observance with those in authority. There are no fewer than six accounts of Jesus engaging in acts of healing on the Sabbath and one occasion of him and his disciples being criticized for reaping because they had been plucking grains of wheat to eat as they walked along the road.[37]

In each case the critique levied against Jesus and/or his disciples by those in authority is that they have violated the Sabbath. And, in each case Jesus responds to such criticism with his own from within the tradition of law and custom that inform his critics. A good example of this is recorded in three of the Gospels in the interchange of Jesus around the healing of a man with a withered hand:

> He left that place and entered their synagogue; a man was there with a withered hand, and they asked him, "Is it lawful to cure on the Sabbath?" so that they might accuse him. He said to them, "Suppose one of you has only one sheep and it falls into a pit on the Sabbath; will you not lay hold of it and lift it out? How much more valuable is a human being than a sheep! So it is lawful to do good on the Sabbath." Then he said to the man, "Stretch out your hand." He stretched it out, and it was restored, as sound as the other. (Matthew 12:9-13)

Here in a simple interchange Jesus makes clear the hypocrisy of those who challenge his behavior and in the process reinforces his own understanding of the sanctity of human life, and the centrality of love of neighbor. The indictment against healing comes not as an invitation to a quiet and reflective space in which to rest and reflect upon one's relationship with the Divine, but as a means to restrict Jesus' behavior and to delegitimize his teaching.[38]

Another example of Jesus' use of Torah tradition to support his violation of the indictment against work on the Sabbath can be found in the Gospel of John:

> Jesus answered them, "I performed one work, and all of you are astonished. Moses gave you circumcision [it is, of course, not from Moses, but from the patriarchs], and you circumcise a man on the Sabbath. If a man receives circumcision on the Sabbath in order that the law of Moses may not be broken, are you angry with me because I healed a man's whole body on the Sabbath?" (John 7:21-23)

While this particular text does not give the account of the healing directly, it does bring up the question of healing on the Sabbath and points to an incident we can assume everyone knows about. Jesus equates his healing with the rite of circumcision prescribed in the Torah. This may seem strange, but Jesus is in fact drawing out a sharp comparison of how easily the law is suspended for what is deemed a greater need. He is, in essence, raising the question about the primacy of compassion and mercy (i.e., chesed) by comparing his behavior to the Sabbath in the same light as how circumcision is allowed for on the Sabbath.

SABBATH WAS CREATED FOR HUMANS: WHEN LAWS DON'T SERVE THEIR INTENDED PURPOSE

The ultimate expression of Jesus' motivation for these violations comes in the dialogue, which occurs in Mark over his disciples' behavior on the Sabbath in a wheat field:

> One Sabbath he was going through the wheat fields; and as they made their way his disciples began to pluck heads of grain. The Pharisees said to him, "Look, why are they doing what is not lawful on the Sabbath?" And he said to them, "Have you never read what David did when he and his companions were hungry and in need of food? He entered

the house of God, when Abiathar was high priest, and ate
the bread of the Presence, which it is not lawful for any but
the priests to eat, and he gave some to his companions."
Then he said to them, "The Sabbath was made for
humankind, and not humankind for the Sabbath; so the Son
of Man is lord even of the Sabbath." (Mark 2:23-28)

In this dialogue, again the institutions and structures of power in
the culture (state and temple) are thrown at Jesus as a proof of his
illegitimacy. His response is to talk about a story in the Hebrew
scriptures from the reign of King David that far exceeds the
purported sinfulness of his disciples as a way of dismissing their
charge. But unlike in other encounters, he does not stop simply by
scripturally outmaneuvering the Pharisees. In this particular
encounter Jesus makes plain his understanding of not only Sabbath,
but of the nature of the sacred.

Jesus applies his understanding of scripture to this particular
incident without evasion or subtlety. When taken to its logical
conclusion, Jesus' articulation of the relationship of Sabbath to
humanity leaves all institutions bereft of sacredness. For Jesus,
people are sacred. The sacredness of institutions comes from their
ability to serve the needs of humanity and not the other way
around.

MORALITY IS ABOUT RELATIONSHIPS, NOT RULES

If laws serve only to support an institution's power, or support to
protect and isolate the privileged within an institution, then for
Jesus, such an institution is immoral because its laws, even those
commended by scripture, no longer serve the purpose for which
they were intended.

It is this understanding that brings to articulation the theme that
this chapter concludes, namely that morality is about relationships
and not rules. While systems of ethics can be built on any agreed

upon set of rules that minimize human anxiety and secure a sense of stability within a culture, morality is intrinsically bound up in the sacredness of human life and in the sacred nature of human relationships. Any rule, regardless of its explicit intent, that violates, demeans, or diminishes human life is immoral because it is an affront to the Divine within all of humanity.

How interesting that this is the message of Jesus in light of the pattern of Christian behavior over the last two millennia. In many examples, today's fundamentalism being the most imminent, the notion of a relational morality that puts the good of people over serving an institution (e.g., church, scripture, state, etc.) has become something that is conspicuously absent. Such values are more often than not associated with humanism and liberalism rather than with the practice of faith. In the cases where people of faith do practice such behaviors they are often held suspect by both the religious right and secular liberals as being something outside the norms of Christian practice.

But it is this very practice that leads to the final theme we will consider in this book. The four themes we have examined coalesce into a comprehensive vision of human society in which the Divine is a lived reality. Jesus' term for that vision was "the kingdom of God."

PART VI:
THE KINGDOM OF GOD IS AT HAND

CHAPTER 18:
WHAT IS THE KINGDOM OF GOD?

Whether called the "kingdom of God" or the "kingdom of Heaven," throughout the Gospels Jesus again and again proclaims that this kingdom is at hand, has come near, or is within. It is at the heart of his proclamation and is what he meant when he spoke of the "good news."[39]

We now live in an age when kingship and kingdoms are of little relevance. For most of us, the only notion of royalty that we might have is the Queen of England or the mythical King Arthur. Neither of those images, however, comes close to the vision articulated by Jesus. For this reason the notion of a kingdom of God is, at best, difficult for us.

KING AND KINGDOM: A FIRST CENTURY PERSPECTIVE

The images of king and kingdom out of which Jesus operated are so alien to most modern Westerners as to render them obsolete. If our only images of monarchy are akin to those mentioned earlier, the term is in more danger of miscommunication than of conveying any deep or genuine meaning. Moreover, the radical nature of Jesus' message and the images he attaches to it are completely lost.

Monarchy, as it existed in the ancient world, has not been in common usage in the Western world for centuries. Even the best-known surviving monarchies of the West (including those of Scandinavia, Great Britain, Belgium, and the Netherlands) are, generally speaking, constitutional monarchies with national affairs being largely determined by a constitutionally elected representative body. To truly understand the radical nature of Jesus' image of the kingdom of Heaven, we must first understand the political reality out of which his vision arose.

As we mentioned in the chapters 15 and 16, the primary model of governance in the ancient world could best be described as a system of domination. Power was most often vested in the hands of an individual (monarch) and/or a relatively small group of individuals (nobility). Those who were invested with this authority determined all substantive decisions about the nature of life and the material goods of life.

This meant that Kings had the right to levy taxes, to assemble armies, to distribute wealth, and to enact and enforce laws. The idea was that it then became the obligation of that monarch to ensure the common good and to create a stable environment by which everyone benefited.

As any cursory examination history will attest, more often than not monarchies such as this, to a greater or lesser degree, failed to live fully into such a high view of their obligations. Instead, monarchs were often focused on appeasing the wealthy elites within their kingdoms in order to reinforce their own position and power. In such systems there was vast disparity between wealth and poverty. Examples abound from both antiquity and medieval Europe of significant portions of wealth lying in relatively few hands creating a vast disparity between those who had the material and means of wealth and those who did not.

Monarchs in the ancient world ruled without fear of repercussion, except possibly from an alienated nobility. Since the instruments of control (economic and military) were in the hands of the monarch and those who benefited from the domination system, nothing short of total rebellion (i.e., a peasant revolt) would result in the monarch's reign being interrupted.

Further, monarchs were more often than not, imputed with divine attributes and often given divine titles. They regularly fulfilled not only civil but also religious roles within a society's culture. Most of the titles which early Christians ascribed to Jesus, and which now are understood exclusively as religious terms, were titles that were held by the Emperor of Rome. Augustus was seen as savior, great high priest, and redeemer of the people.

These titles were given to him because of military victory and the securing of Roman peace through conquest. His domination of the Mediterranean world through military means and an effective bureaucracy insured that the citizens of Rome experienced prosperity at a level not seen before. It was the domination system applied on a continental level. As a number of scholars have shown, to use these titles for Jesus was as much a political action and rejection of the domination system of Rome as much as it was an act of adoration for Jesus.

YAHWEH IS OUR KING: BIBLICAL MONARCHY AND THE KINGSHIP OF THE DIVINE

When we look at the biblical narrative in the Hebrew scriptures what we find is a tradition that is suspicious of domination systems, and most specifically of monarchy. Until the elevation of Saul to the kingship of the Israel in the 11th century BCE, there is a strong resistance to monarchy or overt domination systems of government.

This is due to a basic assumption that kingship belongs to the Divine. Repeatedly throughout the books of the Hebrew Scriptures the kingship of the Yahweh[40] in both nature and history is affirmed.

This is especially true in the Psalms and the Prophets. Yahweh is seen as an all-powerful and all-transcendent being who is beyond compare. In this worldview the Divine is marked by tremendous majesty, awe, and power.[41] Similarly, just as Yahweh's nature was not to be compromised by likeness to any created thing (Exodus 20:4), so his lordship was not to be shared with, or usurped by, any human ruler.[42] It is for this reason that ancient Israelites go through a long and drawn out process to monarchy.

Even when there is a single leader such as Moses, leaders before Saul do not function as a monarch, but instead as a servant to the true monarch (Yahweh). Even after Saul, monarchs of both Israel (the northern kingdom) and Judah (the southern kingdom) are seen as monarchs only in that they serve the will of Yahweh. As is shown in the story of Saul, disobedience to Yahweh can result in being dethroned. It is affirmed over and over that the only true monarch is the Divine. It may be shocking to us, as modern people, that most ancient peoples could not imagine any other system of governance than a domination system,[43] but it was a radical step to shift the role of the monarch away from a human figure and to the Divine.

With the Divine as monarch, questions of the well-being of the population are potentially resolved. In fact, moving to the Divine as monarch is an overt attempt to abandon domination systems. Since the behavior of the Divine's nature is chesed, the image of the Divine as king is not one of control and domination but of care, mercy, nurture, and faithfulness. Further, (at least in theory) those who governed now do not serve their own interests, or the interests of the elite but are compelled to serve the interests of the Divine, whose principal nature, as we just said, is chesed.

Needless to say, the advent of monarchy in ancient Israel brought all the common woes of domination systems. This inevitable corruption resulted in the development of the tradition of prophecy in ancient Israel.

Contrary to the popular understanding of the word, prophecy in the biblical narrative has nothing to do with looking into the future and divining cataclysmic events. Instead, prophecy was a response to the domination system's corruption and abuse in the life of ancient Israel and Judah. Groups of faithful people gathered together to focus specifically on the principles by which a society, based on the kingship of Yahweh, would function. Such an orientation allowed gatherings of social critics (i.e., schools of prophecy) and their leaders (i.e., prophets) to critique monarchies and the societies they governed. Prophets used the language of covenant (i.e., blessing and curse) as a means of describing how the society and those who governed failed to meet the standards of Yahweh's kingship. Over and again issues of social, economic, and legal justice sit at the heart of the prophetic tradition. Whether it is the plight of the poor or the dispossessed, or the indifference of the wealthy and the corruption of the monarchy, prophets offered pointed critique, couched in terms of the Divine. Using such language, these ancient social pundits offered warnings of the organic consequences of continued destructive behavior and the benefits of changing to a model in which the chesed of God is embodied in the society.

THE KINGDOM OF GOD: JESUS' ARTICULATION OF THE DIVINE VISION OF HUMANITY

It is out of this prophetic tradition that Jesus' articulation of the kingdom of God is expressed. But, Jesus does not simply repeat the assertions of the kingship of the Divine and critique the social order he encounters. Instead, coming from the understandings expressed in the themes we have already explored he takes the idea of the kingship of Yahweh and shifts the emphasis from the expectations of the Divine to the shape of life in the human community and what a society based on chesed would look like. This is an important point. Jesus does not focus on proclaiming the kingship of the Divine. Instead he proclaims and lives out a vision for the human community based upon the sacredness of people, and the sacred nature of human relationship.

There are 48 instances in the Gospels where Jesus uses the term "kingdom of God" and another 30 where the term "kingdom of Heaven" is used. Combined, the number of references to such an ideal is monumental. It clearly was a central concept for Jesus and a central idea that shaped and formed those who followed him. Why else would it be so present in the presentation of the shape of his life? For our purposes we will presume that the terms "kingdom of God" and "kingdom of Heaven" are synonymous. To make the examination of this concept manageable we will look at three of the parables of Jesus regarding the kingdom of God as a means of unearthing the reality to which it points.

The image of the kingdom of God, which has become well known in our post-modern Western society, is one that is focused on some supernatural kingdom that will be imposed on the created order at the end of time. It has at its core an image of heaven being made on Earth that occurs after a period of cataclysmic proportion, and involves a miraculous city descending from the clouds and the faithful who have died being restored to a bodily existence. While this image has been popular for centuries and is currently the image embraced by fundamentalist interpretations of the Book of Revelation, it has little to do with the image of the kingdom of God found in the Gospels.

Jesus' notion of the kingdom of God appears to be bound up in the prophetic tradition and embraces the idea that the ways in which we live determine how fully we can consciously experience existence in the presence of the Divine. Implicit in Jesus' statements about the kingdom of God is a question. What would the world look like if we actually lived out a principle of steadfast love and faithfulness? How would human existence change if that notion were applied not only to our spirituality, but also to the relationships we have with every human being (our friends, our family, our neighbors, the stranger, and even our enemies)?

Jesus' use of the term "kingdom of God" was a means of conveying and reinterpreting the notion of Yahweh's kingship into a model of understanding how each and every human life is sacred and, by extension, every relationship is also sacred. It is a way of thinking about the sovereignty of the Divine that puts the emphasis not on myth and metaphor but on the tangible in our lives, and marks the spiritual mystery to be found in that tangibility. To make this point we turn to three parables, which express the deeply sacred and relational nature of human life.

The Parable of the Lost Sheep

While the kingdom of God is not explicitly mentioned in this particular parable it comes in the context of Jesus teaching about "entering into life" and in the wake of having scolded the disciples about their treatment of children. To this end, it seems clear that this parable speaks to his understanding of human relationship and the nature of the kingdom of God.

> "Take care that you do not despise one of these little ones; for, I tell you, in heaven their angels continually see the face of my Father in heaven. What do you think? If a shepherd has a hundred sheep, and one of them has gone astray, does he not leave the ninety-nine on the mountains and go in search of the one that went astray? And if he finds it, truly I tell you, he rejoices over it more than over the ninety-nine that never went astray. So it is not the will of your Father in heaven that one of these little ones should be lost." (Matthew 18:10-14)

For Jesus, the nature of the Divine is found in the importance and sacredness of each individual. The good of the many does not outweigh the good of the one. In the kingdom of God each and every person, regardless of any other factor, is of value.

The Parable of the Forgiving Father

This particular parable is especially poignant as an expression about the multiple dimensions of the sacred nature of human relationship and the complexities that arise out of such relationships. The father and the two sons paint a sophisticated psychological triangle out of which a number of common dynamics continue to be played out. It is a very human drama marked by deeply spiritual themes.

> Then Jesus said, "There was a man who had two sons. The younger of them said to his father, 'Father, give me the share of the property that will belong to me.' So he divided his property between them. A few days later the younger son gathered all he had and traveled to a distant country, and there he squandered his property in dissolute living. When he had spent everything, a severe famine took place throughout that country, and he began to be in need. So he went and hired himself out to one of the citizens of that country, who sent him to his fields to feed the pigs. He would gladly have filled himself with the pods that the pigs were eating; and no one gave him anything. But when he came to himself he said, 'How many of my father's hired hands have bread enough and to spare, but here I am dying of hunger! I will get up and go to my father, and I will say to him, 'Father, I have sinned against heaven and before you; I am no longer worthy to be called your son; treat me like one of your hired hands.' So he set off and went to his father. But while he was still far off, his father saw him and was filled with compassion; he ran and put his arms around him and kissed him. Then the son said to him, 'Father, I have sinned against heaven and before you; I am no longer worthy to be called your son.' But the father said to his slaves, 'Quickly, bring out a robe—the best one—and put it on him; put a ring on his finger and sandals on his feet. And get the fatted calf and kill it, and let us eat and

celebrate; for this son of mine was dead and is alive again; he was lost and is found!' And they began to celebrate. Now his elder son was in the field; and when he came and approached the house, he heard music and dancing. He called one of the slaves and asked what was going on. He replied, 'Your brother has come, and your father has killed the fatted calf, because he has got him back safe and sound.' Then he became angry and refused to go in. His father came out and began to plead with him. But he answered his father, 'Listen! For all these years I have been working like a slave for you, and I have never disobeyed your command; yet you have never given me even a young goat so that I might celebrate with my friends. But when this son of yours came back, who has devoured your property with prostitutes, you killed the fatted calf for him!' Then the father said to him, 'Son, you are always with me, and all that is mine is yours. But we had to celebrate and rejoice, because this brother of yours was dead and has come to life; he was lost and has been found.'" (Luke 15:11-32)

This story points to questions of faithfulness, forgiveness, justice, mercy, stewardship of one's resources, and care of one's relationships. It presents the messiness of life and all its emotional complexities while offering a beautiful and poignant glimpse into a realized concept of chesed. Such behavior speaks to Jesus' understanding of the kingdom of God.

The Parable of the Separating of Sheep and Goats

The last of the parables we review comes as the clearest statement of the sacredness of people. In this parable humanity is divided into sheep and goats (symbols of righteousness and defilement). Those who are righteous (e.g, in right relationship to the Divine) are commended for their acts of chesed to the Divine, while those who are deemed defiled are condemned for their indifference to the Divine.

"When the Son of Man comes in his glory, and all the angels with him, then he will sit on the throne of his glory. All the nations will be gathered before him, and he will separate people one from another as a shepherd separates the sheep from the goats, and he will put the sheep at his right hand and the goats at the left. Then the king will say to those at his right hand, 'Come, you that are blessed by my Father, inherit the kingdom prepared for you from the foundation of the world; for I was hungry and you gave me food, I was thirsty and you gave me something to drink, I was a stranger and you welcomed me, I was naked and you gave me clothing, I was sick and you took care of me, I was in prison and you visited me.' Then the righteous will answer him, 'Lord, when was it that we saw you hungry and gave you food, or thirsty and gave you something to drink? And when was it that we saw you a stranger and welcomed you, or naked and gave you clothing? And when was it that we saw you sick or in prison and visited you?' And the king will answer them, 'Truly I tell you, just as you did it to one of the least of these who are members of my family, you did it to me.' Then he will say to those at his left hand, 'You that are accursed, depart from me into the eternal fire prepared for the devil and his angels; for I was hungry and you gave me no food, I was thirsty and you gave me nothing to drink, I was a stranger and you did not welcome me, naked and you did not give me clothing, sick and in prison and you did not visit me.' Then they also will answer, 'Lord, when was it that we saw you hungry or thirsty or a stranger or naked or sick or in prison, and did not take care of you?' Then he will answer them, 'Truly I tell you, just as you did not do it to one of the least of these, you did not do it to me.' And these will go away into eternal punishment, but the righteous into eternal life." (Matthew 25:31-46)

The ironic twist to those who first heard this, as to most of us now, is that service of the Divine has nothing to do with religious observance, spirituality, or belief. Rather, service of the Divine is seen in terms of the service of fellow human beings, specifically, service to those within the human community who are "the least" (meaning those in greatest need or who have been most marginalized by the larger culture). For Jesus, there is no question how one knows the Divine. The Divine is known in the context of human relationship and the kingdom of God is human relationships marked by conscious mutuality, steadfastness, and love. It is in this context that the reality of the Divine will become explicit and the kingdom of Heaven will appear. Put succinctly, the kingdom of God is the Divine vision of humanity, it is the notion of humanity living in a commonwealth of peace and justice in which all are free to live to their potential and the needs of all are met by all.

CHAPTER 19:
"AT HAND" AND "WITHIN" -
METAPHORS FOR HUMAN AGENCY

As we have already discovered in the previous chapter, Jesus proclaimed the kingdom of God as a divine vision of the human community marked by the characteristics of peace, justice, steadfast love, and faithfulness. But simply to end the discussion there would be to miss the tension his proclamation created within his own context and still creates today. It is a tension that Jesus spoke to directly, and challenges one of the most dominant assumptions in many different faith practices today.

All we need to do to recognize this tension is to ask ourselves: Where have we seen this kingdom of God? And moreover, even if we accept that it is an inherently human expression in which the Divine is revealed, how do we recognize it when it is expressed? There seem to be no shortage of competing and conflicting interpretations of what the kingdom of God is and where it is to be found. For some, this kingdom is something that will only be known when this life is over, for others it was expressed in the life of Jesus and needs to be modeled now, and for still others it is something for which we strive trusting that the Divine will usher it in at some point in the future.

These tensions are very similar to the ones that confronted Jesus among the people with whom he lived, worked, and loved. Why has God abandoned us to the Romans? When will Israel be restored? When will God's reign begin and injustice end? Is it something that we will only know after death? Is it something breaking into this life? Is it something that God will establish at some point in the future? To these questions Jesus has two responses: The kingdom of God is within you, and the kingdom of God is at hand.

THE KINGDOM OF GOD IS WITHIN YOU: FINDING THE DIVINE VISION

In the Gospel of Luke Jesus is confronted with a question by the Pharisees asking him about the kingdom of God:

> Once Jesus was asked by the Pharisees when the kingdom of God was coming, and he answered, "The kingdom of God is not coming with things that can be observed; nor will they say, 'Look, here it is!' or 'There it is!' For, in fact, the kingdom of God is among you." (Luke 17:20-21)

While the motivations of the Pharisee cannot be known, this dialogue is marked by a genuine question asked out the tradition from which Jesus speaks. The notion of the kingdom of God was, in Jesus' time, understood to be about the restoration of Israel by the Divine. It was, if you will, a metaphor for the idealized Israelite state. And so, when the Pharisees ask this question, there is nothing in it that can be construed as facetious or disingenuous. It is a question that many people who had heard Jesus' regular proclamation about the kingdom of God would have been wondering.

But Jesus' reply conveys a very different understanding from that of the popular wisdom of his day. It points to the understanding of kingdom of God that we have already discussed in the prior chapter, but goes on to elucidate the nature of the kingdom as a vision and where such a vision comes.

Rather than being the establishment of a kingdom marked by signs and wonders, or by political and military action, it is something that wells up within the individual. It is made manifest in the internal reality of each human being. This kingdom therefore is not a system that will be imposed on humanity as a saving grace, because to do so would be to simply replace one domination system with another.

No, the kingdom is an expression of consciousness on the part of each human being. It is a vision that comes from within and is an expression of the Divine within the life force of each person. It is something that arises within us and to which we arise. It is the expression of hope and the commitment to chesed.

In other words, the kingdom of God is both about how we orient ourselves to the world around us and about how we choose to behave in order to make that reality something we share with others. For those who have embraced the vision no collective agreement is needed, no covenant mandated. For those who look for the kingdom outside of themselves no collective agreement is sufficient, no covenant enforceable.

THE KINGDOM OF GOD IS AT HAND: RECOGNIZING THE POTENTIAL FOR KINGDOM LIVING

But while Jesus was clearly convinced of the internal reality of the kingdom of God, he equally regularly proclaimed its nearness. Whether using the term "at hand" or "come near,"[44] Jesus not only proclaims the radical nearness of the kingdom but instructs his followers to do likewise. Further it is this message, the nearness of the kingdom of God, which he understands to be the "good news."

Why would the nearness of the kingdom be good news? It is a worthy question to ask. Is it because of the implied nearness of the

Divine and perhaps a rescue from all that ails humanity? Is it because the nearness of the kingdom implies the closeness of the end of injustice? Perhaps. But, taking all that we have examined up to this point into account, it seems clearer that the kingdom's nearness is good news because it is possible to experience it and is not something for which we must wait.

By proclaiming that the kingdom is at hand, Jesus is communicating that the reality of the Divine vision for humanity is, quite literally, within our reach. It is an amazing idea. Much like we would say today, when we say something is at hand, Jesus is pushing us to recognize how intimately we are already involved in the reality of the kingdom of God. It is an invitation to recognize the radical imminence of the Divine in our lives and an invitation to participate in it.

Jesus' proclamation of the nearness of the kingdom on several occasions comes in response to the behaviors of others. Whether it is the hospitality of those who receive his followers when they are sent out (Luke 9:1-6), healing has occurred (Luke 9:11), or the chesed understanding of law expressed by the scribe (Matthew 12:32-34), Jesus proclaims that in light of such behaviors one is to proclaim the nearness of the kingdom of God.

When taken with the parables Jesus told, the image of the nearness of the kingdom is an invitation to recognize the importance of human agency. In response to those who expected the kingdom of God to appear immediately Jesus told this parable:

> "A nobleman went to a distant country to get royal power for himself and then return. He summoned ten of his slaves, and gave them ten talents, and said to them, 'Do business with these until I come back.' But the citizens of his country hated him and sent a delegation after him, saying, 'We do not want this man to rule over us.' When he returned, having received royal power, he ordered these slaves, to whom he had given the money, to be summoned so that he

might find out what they had gained by trading. The first came forward and said, 'Lord, your pound has made ten more pounds.' He said to him, 'Well-done, good slave! Because you have been trustworthy in a very small thing, take charge of ten cities.' Then the second came, saying, 'Lord, your pound has made five pounds.' He said to him, 'And you, rule over five cities.' Then the other came, saying, 'Lord, here is your pound. I wrapped it up in a piece of cloth, for I was afraid of you, because you are a harsh man; you take what you did not deposit, and reap what you did not sow.' He said to him, 'I will judge you by your own words, you wicked slave! You knew, did you, that I was a harsh man, taking what I did not deposit and reaping what I did not sow? Why then did you not put my money into the bank? Then when I returned, I could have collected it with interest.' He said to the bystanders, 'Take the pound from him and give it to the one who has ten pounds.' (And they said to him, 'Lord, he has ten pounds!') 'I tell you, to all those who have, more will be given; but from those who have nothing, even what they have will be taken away." (Luke 19:11-27)

While out of context this parable might be seen as a strange story about investment and the wrath of the Divine against fearful hoarding, in its proper context we can see that it is a response to passivity in terms of Jesus' kingdom proclamation. The three slaves' own behavior represents their willingness to engage the reality that is before them, to recognize the richness of the experience that has been afforded them, and to take the risks associated with such abundance. The analogy one might make from such a reading is that the third slave's sin is not that he did not make a profit, but that he did not take the risk, nor did he recognize the rich experience that had been offered to him. It seems possible that, were we able to engage Jesus about this teaching, he might well make it clear that to those who risk there is equal reward for both success and failure. Given that Jesus rejected materialism as a valid mode of understanding the value of life, it seems highly unlikely that his intent in this story is simply to say that the kingdom of God is based upon material success.

Rather, in light of this parable, the invitation is one to active engagement with the kingdom that is always within one's grasp. It is an invitation to recognize the vision from within, to rise up to its challenge, and then to embrace and step into the opportunities that arise on a daily basis. It is the paradox of such living to which we turn in the final chapter of this section.

CHAPTER 20:
ALWAYS AND NEVER

There are significant implications from our study of Jesus' notion of the kingdom of God and his use of "at hand" and "within you." Placed within the context of our larger reflection on the core themes explored earlier, Jesus places the idea of the in-breaking (i.e., imminence) of God into human affairs into a very different place than Christianity has as a religion for most of the last 2,000 years. In fact, with further examination, one can fairly say that the whole notion of how, when, and why God appears in the human story has been misinterpreted for millennia. To begin to crack the puzzle as to why that is, we start by looking at the frame from which we have understood the notion of the kingdom for much of the history of Christianity.

ESCHATOLOGY: THE STUDY OF ENDINGS

The theological term given for the in-breaking of the kingdom of God and the end of the social order as we have it is called "eschatology." Eschatology is a Greek word that means "the study of (logos) the end (eschatos)." Within the field of Christian theology specifically, it has generally come to be understood as "the doctrine of the last things, that is the ultimate destiny both of the individual soul and the whole created order."[45]

To one degree or another and for most of the history of Christianity, practitioners of the Christian faith have generally agreed that Jesus' references to the kingdom of God have pointed to the "end times." There has been, and continues to be in many parts of Christianity (notably Catholic and evangelical fundamentalism), a belief that the references to the kingdom of God are a reference to an actual kingdom that will be made manifest on Earth at the end of all time. These expressions of the Christian faith await expectantly the return of a triumphant Christ who will ride in on a white charger from the sky with avenging angels that will reward the righteous and punish the wicked. It will be the end of everything that plagues the human condition and the Earth will once again become an Eden in which humanity and the Divine will live in perfect harmony. In such a vision, dogged obedience to the commandments of scripture, and the enforcement of those commandments upon those who violate them, are the hallmarks of righteousness.

Such a theology sees this life as a testing ground for how well one can live in accordance with God's will and that it is of value only in that it serves that purpose. For this reason, many conservative Christian traditions today do not place a high value on environmental stewardship, eliminating wealth inequality, issues of gender equality, the reduction of war and violence, or the protection of the rights of individuals. Instead, this theology sees such issues as being within the purview of the Divine and outside the mandates for human living. Such individuals strive to meet the commandments as they understand them and wait passively for salvation to occur. Further, such salvation is often seen as a wholly individual and personal matter with little to no communal dimension. The implication of such individualism is that there is no sense of collective responsibility for anything that may, even from their own theological understanding, be a violation of the commandments of the Divine.

It is such a paradigm that has led to many of the greatest atrocities in the history of Christianity (e.g., the Crusades, the Inquisition, the witch trials of the 16th and 17th centuries, the persecution of science and scientists, countless pogroms against Jews, etc.). When we are freed from the demands of the world and responsibility to our neighbor, and live exclusively in a spiritualized reality that sees little value in others or the world around oneself, then morality becomes so narrowly defined as to allow indifference to suffering, or worse, grossly immoral acts to be perpetrated in the name of faith.

But the other tragedy of such a theology is that it is a human existence bereft of the presence of the Divine. The Divine is, at best, known only by proxy through the mediation of an institution (i.e., the church). The deep craving for the Divine that continued in humanity was relegated to the superstitious elevation of the bread and wine of Holy Communion to a divine status, rather than recognizing that its ability to connect us with the Divine comes through communion with one another and in the very human interdependent act of meal sharing. Instead, throughout the Middle Ages, and even today in some places, the bread blessed for sharing in communion is instead placed under glass and elevated above people so that it can be adored as the Divine. Such a practice can only arise when one presumes that the Divine is distant and unavailable until his return at the end of time.

This is just one example of any number of developments in both Catholic and Protestant theology that develop out of an eschatology that awaits the end of the world and the return of Christ. But there is an alternative that we can detect out of the work we have done, one that Christian theologians, starting in the 19th century, began to identify. It is an approach that arises out of the five themes and calls us to a different understanding of Jesus own vision of eschatology.

THE END OF TIME RATHER THAN THE END TIMES

In the last chapter we explored Jesus' notion that the kingdom of God is within each and every one of us. He made this proclamation in Jerusalem in response to the anticipation of those gathered that the kingdom would be coming immediately. More specifically, he was responding to the understanding that it was something that would be observed by us rather than enacted by us, that it was a passive reality rather than an active one.

Jesus' proclamation that the kingdom is within us indicates that what we have been waiting for has been with us all along and yet we fail to experience it because we are waiting for it to come as a passive reality in the future. It is a direct critique to the theology that developed after him (ironically in his name!?!). His understanding of the coming of the kingdom of God is based on a non-linear understanding of time. It is based upon the first of our themes, that all there is is now. It is a proclamation that time is ended and that the kingdom of God is with us now.

Jesus challenges his followers and us to claim a very different understanding of reality than most of us grew up with, whether we are people of faith or not. It is the understanding that the only reality there is is the one we claim. It is an understanding that whatever there is that is sacred can only be found in the now and in the context of human relationships. It is a vision of divinity and humanity that is intertwined inextricably. It is a vision of the world and of human society that exceeds the greatest expectations we have ever placed upon ourselves and at the same time recognizes and accepts our limitations. It is what the biblical theologian John Dominic Crossan calls a "realized eschatology."[46]

Such an eschatology places an emphasis on the shape of the life of Jesus and on his teaching as a means of engaging his mystical understanding of the kingdom of God. It is a way of embracing Jesus' own understanding that the Divine is always within our grasp and is always to be found in human relationships. It sets aside worship and scripture as the central aspects of Christian identity while not abandoning them. It allows for a practice of the Christian faith that is open and inclusive to other traditions, because, as its central tenet, it is "seeking and serving Christ in all persons" and striving to "love one's neighbor as one's self."[47]

THE PARADOX: ALWAYS AND NEVER

Such an approach genuinely creates a paradox for life, however. The reality of living as Jesus presents means that we simultaneously live with the vibrant presence of the Divine in our lives and are able to recognize, again and again, the ways in which the human community expresses this divine presence. But, such a reality also creates within us the ability to recognize equally the myriad ways in which the reality of the Divine is violated within the human context and undermined over and over through indifference and injustice. It further allows us to recognize those areas of life in which we either respect the Earth as the context in which this drama is played out or abuse it.

Such a paradox can be seen as a burden we must bear, but we are only tempted to understand this reality as a burden when we long for an idyllic past that never existed, a utopian future that will never exist, or wish to be a passive observer and wait for the Divine to intervene.

Instead, the functional reality of Jesus' message is that the divine vision of the human community, the commonwealth of peace and justice that is the kingdom of God, is always present should we be willing to reach for what is within our grasp. It is a reality that will animate and sustain us if we are but willing to embrace that which is at hand and do what needs to be done regardless of demand or cost.

On the other hand, there is an equal functional warning that we will be perpetually frustrated and alienated from that commonwealth of peace and justice if we understand it as a static reality, one that can be achieved and sustained without our individual effort. Or worse, it will be a false vision that will undermine our efforts if we see it as something that will simply be bestowed upon us by the Divine because of our moralistic or pietistic behavior.

For Jesus, the kingdom of God is the encapsulation of the first four themes we have explored. It is the vision of what the world looks like when we live out of those themes. It is a clarion call to embrace both the Divine and our divine calling.

PART VII:
A POST-NICENE CHRISTIANITY

CHAPTER 21:
WAS JESUS A TEACHER OF SUTRAS?

THE WESTERN JESUS: CAN HE BE FOUND?

Having now come to the end of the five themes (sutras) that were outlined at the beginning of this book we are left with the question, was Jesus a teacher of sutras? To answer that question, let's start by looking at the four presuppositions of Western models and see if any of them apply to the Jesus we have just encountered.

As a reminder, the four presuppositions are that Western models of teaching: (1) tend to focus on individual identity, (2) tend to a mechanistic worldview, (3) are based on the assumption of the inevitability of conflict, and (4) tend to focus on the ideal.

Did Jesus focus on individual identity?

While there are many stories that involve the individual, and Jesus was willing to engage individual persons, it is clear from the preponderance of the material that Jesus always dealt with the individual within the context of a community. His principal images were familial and communal, and rarely, if ever, focused on the individual as a separate and autonomous unit. In short, Jesus was not all that focused on individual identity.

Was Jesus mechanistic in his worldview?

Reviewing the material examined, as well as the Gospels in general, there is a dearth of material that can be described as mechanistic. Mechanical metaphors are nowhere to be found, nor does Jesus seem all that interested in mathematical or mechanical approaches to the question of sin and forgiveness. So again, the simple answer is no, Jesus did not have a mechanistic worldview.

Did Jesus assume the inevitability of conflict?

This question is a little different and the answer is not as simple. It seems clear that Jesus did actually presume the inevitability of some kinds of conflict. He saw a basic conflict between the divine vision for humanity and the domination systems (both political and religious) that were firmly ensconced. This is expressed quintessentially in Matthew 10:34 where Jesus says, "I did not come to bring peace, but a sword." In this regard, it seems clear that Jesus looks more Western in his worldview, but when we look at his teaching in the context of such statements, he does not presume that the response to such discord is further conflict.

It seems clear that Jesus was principally focused on love (chesed) as a principal behavior. This would differentiate his position from dominant Western models, which presume mutual conflict as normative. Rather, Jesus' model abandons a win-lose paradigm and instead invites an alternative response. This is best expressed in chapter 13 of the Gospel of John where Jesus washes the disciples' feet, including those of his betrayer (Judas). In that passage, even as he prepares himself for the traumatic events ahead, he models for others the pattern of chesed in the face of conflict.

So the answer to this question is a qualified yes, recognizing that while he accepts conflict as a reality, he invites an alternative response to conflict.

Was Jesus focused on the ideal?

Whether talking about concepts of love, justice, mercy, or neighbor, Jesus repeatedly speaks to the reality of people's lives rather than to some ideal to which he believes they ought to live. His parables are consistently focused on images that are part of the ordinary and mundane realities of life. And while he preaches the kingdom of God and its nearness, he does not envision a utopian society filled with a perfected humanity. Instead, the kingdom of God is the reality that is always within our grasp if we choose to lean into it; it is a reality that is neither passively nor ideally presented. For Jesus, the focus is not on the ideal, but on the reality of the Divine in our lives as they are.

IS THERE EVIDENCE FOR AN EASTERN JESUS?

Clearly then, with three noes and only one qualified yes, that leaves us with a Jesus whose teaching model does not neatly fit into the presuppositions of Western teaching. But, does he fit an Eastern model? A similar review of the presuppositions of an Eastern model of teaching should help to clarify the matter.

Again, as a reminder, the four presuppositions of an Eastern model of teaching are that Eastern models: (1) tend to focus on communal identity (2) tend to an organic worldview, (3) are based on harmony as a principal motivation and (4) tend to be pragmatic rather than ideal.

Did Jesus focus on communal identity?

Whether looking at his relational ethics or his familial imagery of the Divine, Jesus does not see anyone in an individualistic way. This is no surprise as it is part and parcel of the prophetic tradition out of which he is formed and teaches. Again, Jesus does not understand his own life, the life of others, or the life of the Divine apart from community. As we have seen repeatedly, for Jesus, all of reality is relational in nature. His core message about the imminence of the kingdom of God cannot be adequately understood unless it is seen within a communal context. Communal identity is not simply about how we behave, but also about how we come to understand ourselves.

Was Jesus organic in his worldview?

Jesus was inherently organic in his worldview. Images of nature and the natural order abound in his parables and his speaking. His own sense of morality and how one relates to the Divine were not abstracted, but instead were shaped by the environment in which he found himself.. He did not reduce religious or moral observance to mechanical obedience to an arbitrary set of rules. Rather, Jesus lives in a world in which the Divine makes the rain to sun shine on both the good and the bad. He lives in a world in which suffering is the natural consequence of one's behavior. Again, Jesus had a deeply organic worldview.

Did Jesus promote harmony as a principal motivation?

While, as we have already discussed, Jesus accepted the reality of conflict in the world as inevitable, it seems clear that he did not accept conflict as a principal motivation. Nor did he accept aggression or conflict escalation as a normative response. At the heart of all of Jesus' teaching is the assumption of the chesed of God and the ability of humanity to express chesed to one another. It is this realized act of love and justice, both in the doing and in the receiving, that becomes the principal motivation for all of human life and endeavor. It is a vision of the human community living out of chesed that becomes expressed by Jesus as the kingdom of God. The kingdom of God becomes a compelling vision of a commonwealth of peace and justice in which the needs of all are met by all. It is this vision of humanity in harmony with one another and the Divine that becomes the principal good news he proclaims.

Was Jesus pragmatic rather than ideal?

While it has become quite popular to idealize the teachings of Jesus, we have seen in multiple examinations throughout this book that Jesus was less concerned with an idealized Divine, an idealized moral code, or an idealized religion, than he was with the reality of the Divine in people's real lives. It is the radical accessibility of God and the radical placement of that accessibility in ordinary life that contributed to the large numbers of people who were drawn to him. We have seen how Jesus presented a simple and pragmatic approach to living that gives one access to the sacred without having to be perfect or to beat ourselves up for our shortcomings. In some regards, the simplicity of this message was too good to be true for those who would come later. We will explore in the next chapter how Jesus' message was subverted to dominant models that allowed for anxiety reduction. Nonetheless, Jesus appears less concerned with an ideal than with the reality of the lives he encountered, and even less concerned with an idealized God rather than the lived experience of the Divine in his life and the lives of others.

DOING JUSTICE TO THE EASTERN JESUS

So, after such an examination, it is clear that we have a Jesus that is far more Eastern than Western. One might argue there is so little of Western presupposition in his behavior and teaching that it is an act of violence to have westernized him as thoroughly as our culture has.

It is fair to say that Jesus is a sutric teacher. But it is equally important to point out that he was not a Hindu, nor was he a Buddhist. Jesus was a Jew. His Eastern sensibilities arose out of the prophetic and mystical traditions in which he was formed. His enlightenment came out of Jewish tradition and not some other. Those who would argue that Jesus must have been exposed to Buddhism or Hinduism are resorting to unnecessary speculation.

We have seen more than enough evidence in our examination of the biblical texts to know that Jesus' Eastern orientation needs no other source than his own tradition.

This recognition that Jesus is not Western is an essential step, however, in recovering the Christ that the Church has forgotten. Without such recognition, we are bereft of the power and wonder of this man, who his own followers came to understand as the incarnation of the Divine.

In the last two chapters of this book we will first look at how and why Jesus originally became a Western figure and then chart one possible way of rethinking the practice of Christianity so that it might once again be more in line with the teachings of Jesus.

CHAPTER 22:
ORIGINS OF THE WESTERN JESUS
AND AN ALTERNATIVE

As these themes began to emerge, each one of them hit me like a bolt of lightning. They destabilized my assumptions about the Christian faith while equally undermining the unhelpful images I had of Jesus. But I was little prepared for the impact of all of them together on my faith journey and the implications they collectively bring to the question of faith in the 21st century. But before we turn to the implications of the Jesus we just uncovered, it is worthwhile to turn to the question, "So how exactly did we end up with a predominantly western image of Jesus?"

THE CREEDS: TRIBAL RELIGION MIXED WITH GRECO-ROMAN PHILOSOPHY

For most of the history of Western Christianity we have read the stories of the life of Jesus through what I termed earlier a larger cultural context. To be more exact, much of what the institution of Christianity and those who participated in it did was to take the ecumenical creeds developed between the fourth and sixth centuries of the Common Era and use them as a filter for interpreting the meaning of these sacred stories. Those creeds (i.e., the Apostle's Creed, the Nicene Creed, the declaration of the two

natures of Christ from the Creed of Chalcedon, and the Creed of St. Athanasius) became the principal means by which we understood who and what Jesus was and is. What may be surprising is that those creeds are informed as much, if not more, by Greco-Roman philosophy (e.g., Plato, Aristotle, etc.) than by the witness of scripture.

It was quite shocking for me to learn in the context of my graduate theological education just how deeply these creedal statements were shaped by philosophical thought and language. Further it was a shock to find out that the impetus to create these creedal statements came not from those who were practicing the faith of the church, but by Roman emperors and their governments.

When the emperor Constantine came to power in the fourth century he was impressed by the compassion and civility of those who practiced Christianity. He saw its potential for unifying a diverse and disparate empire. But he was equally concerned at the instability within Christianity and its wide variety of expressions. If Christianity were going to be a unifying institution it would have to have a unified theology and system of organization.

Prior to 325 CE, Christianity had spread throughout the Empire on a grassroots level, always functioning in small groups that met in houses or other private locations. Much like today's denominationalism, there was a whole host of different expressions of Christianity as well. But, unlike today, the breadth and variety of understanding who Jesus was and the significance of his life and message varied greatly. Some theologies would look very familiar to us today, while others would be quite alien.[48]

For this reason Constantine called the first ecumenical council to meet at his villa in the city of Nicea in the year 325 CE. Bishops from all over the Empire were invited (many being forced to attend at spear point) in order to resolve their theological differences. It is not clear whether or not Constantine had a preference of theology, but what was clear was that he wanted there to be only one theology.

The first council of Nicea produced what is now termed the Apostle's Creed. Its primary work was to come to agreement about the relationship of God and Jesus. It is in this controversy between two bishops that the extra-scriptural debate becomes clear. One bishop, Arius, argued that Jesus, if he is divine, was a created being and not co-eternal with the God the Creator. He never questioned Jesus' pre-existence; he simply did not see him as eternal. His argument was that God made the spirit of Jesus and then through Jesus' spirit everything else in Creation was made. He was deeply concerned that to do otherwise was to say that there was more than one God. He therefore argued that Jesus was of a like nature to the Father (in Greek, *homoiousios*). His opponent, Bishop Alexander, argued that if Jesus was the Son of God then he and God the Creator were co-eternal and that Jesus was of the same substance as the Creator (in Greek, *homoousios*). This matter was so contentious as to cause schism and conflict for decades to come and ultimately to result in a state-endorsed persecution of anyone who did not affirm the coeternal nature of Jesus with the Creator.

Needless to say, one can "cherry pick" scriptures to support either position, but the Gospels are not particularly concerned with such a question and so, in the end, it was philosophical argument and debate, and no small amount of politics, that determined the outcome.

Debates such as this continued so that at the second council in Constantinople in 381 CE, the homoousios position was solidified and the question of the Trinity became a hot topic. Jesus' declaration of sending a helper after his departure, and the use of the term Father, Son, and Holy Spirit in several scriptures erupted in debate over the nature of the Holy Spirit and whether it was a product of the Father and Son or a co-eternal and co-equal person of the Trinity.

While there were several councils in between, in 451 CE the last of the major controversies was decided. In this council the raging debate was over whether or not the historical person of Jesus was fully human and then adopted by God (i.e., filled with the second person of the Trinity), fully divine and only appeared to be human (i.e., Docetism), or both fully human and fully divine. Again, while the scriptures can be argued from any of the perspectives the result was to use the language of classical Western philosophy to determine the debate and to choose a single definition.

Isn't it amazing that Jesus' use of the term "father" for the Divine becomes the source of such debate? As we examined earlier in the book, his use of the term was to engender a sense of the radical intimacy of God and emphasize the Divine's orientation of love. But by the fourth century these words had become the fodder for a debate over the nature of Jesus and the relationship of Jesus and the Spirit to the Divine. Rather than understanding "father" as a term that is appropriately used by all humanity it becomes assumed to be the description of a divine family structure.

Furthermore, when one looks at the Apostle and Nicene Creeds the only things of importance about Jesus appear to be his birth, death, and resurrection. Nothing about the substance and shape of his life is mentioned.

Evenso, throughout this debate, the question of power and place within the Empire was what was really at the heart of the matter. One has to ask why such a question becomes so important when, for the first three centuries, the church seemed to be able to exist with radical difference?[49] Put simply, and at least initially, it was a matter of survival. Once the church became a part of the Roman Empire and the agenda for unity was set, the question of who would control that institution, and ultimately who would survive became a driving factor. Differences that were immaterial up to that point became central and theological/philosophical questions of belief became the litmus test for who was in and who was out.

It is interesting to note, that nowhere in our discussion over the last 21 chapters has there been anything about belief being necessary. The central quality of the life Jesus proclaims is chesed (steadfast love, faithfulness, mercy, and justice). And yet, because of the state's need for survival, anxiety reduction, and communal stability, the central characteristic of Christianity from the fourth century forward became determining right belief and defining faith as right belief. This isn't surprising since the Roman agenda from the start was to use the church to bring stability and unity to the Empire. But the unintended consequence of this agenda was to pervert the core teaching of Jesus, so that once again religion served its tribal and primitive purpose as a means of dealing with anticipatory anxiety and fear.

And so, over time we more and more accepted a Western image of Jesus. His teachings, framed under the banner of belief, became yet another layer of data that could be used for determining whether or not one believed correctly. For many, belief in those teachings as discrete facts became the definition of faith and the means of salvation. For centuries following (millennia even), the pattern of church life continued on the path established by imperial bishops of the fourth through sixth centuries. This is not to delegitimize the authenticity of their faith, nor is it to demonize them. Merely, this is to point out that the religion they created, while rooted in the witness of scripture and the person of Jesus, was shaped more by forces other than those to which they hoped to point.

But we now live in an age when supernaturalism and literalism are no longer tenable for a majority of the population. The fear and irrationality of the system created by those imperial bishops is being rejected by ever-increasing numbers of people, including many clergy who find it untenable to preach a religion that is marked by a capricious and indifferent deity.

But, if the themes we have outlined are even remotely true in regard to what Jesus intended—if there is within the shape of the life of this first-century Palestinian preacher something rich and deep worth pursuing—then the implications are significant for Christianity as a faith system, and for each us finding meaning and hope in the 21st century.

RELATIONAL RELIGION: RELEVANT AND HOPEFUL FAITH

So, what exactly are the implications of these five themes? Well, the first and most obvious answer is that Jesus and his teachings are not bound by the tribal assumptions or cultural moralism we have come to associate with him.

These themes invite us to recognize that Jesus was as disinterested in conventional religion as most of us. This does not mean he was not a person of faith, but rather that his faith had a more personal and integral quality to it than what Western Christian tradition might incline us to assume. In light of what we have explored we might expect Jesus in the present context to invite others to be spiritual but not religious. I do think, however, that the Jesus we encounter in these themes would be quick to recognize that religion as a vehicle to spirituality is not the problem. If he were to commend abandoning religion, it would be a critique of how religion in our present context is riddled with anxiety and survival behavior in the same ways that religion in the first century was. He would, as he did then, invite us to explore what living in the eternal now of the Divine is like and then call us to a path of love, justice, mercy, and faithfulness. He would invite us to abandon the animal need for survival and embrace the reality of being adored and connected with all of life and with one another.

The second implication of these themes, as we have just seen, is that the Gospels are incredibly relevant to life today, even as the institutional and doctrinal models of church become increasingly irrelevant. Read with a second naïveté, these stories as they present the shape of the life of Jesus and his teaching, offer relevant and meaningful insight into the mystery of life. They offer a glimpse at dynamics that are as true today as they were in the first century. And, despite the baggage of fourth- through sixth-century imperial theology, as well as medievalism, they are a message of liberation and life to those who take the time to listen and to pattern their lives in a manner that is congruent to the one presented.

Finally, and most significantly, these themes call us to consider another way of being Christian that humanity has forgotten. Through the themes that shaped the message and life of Jesus, we are being called to an evolutionary step beyond traditional religion in which we move from belief in ideas to a relationship with a deeper reality. It is to this idea that we turn in the final chapter of our journey.

CHAPTER 23:
MOVING FROM BELIEF IN IDEAS TO A RELATIONSHIP WITH A DEEPER REALITY

What we have seen, as we have moved through the shape of the life and teaching of Jesus, is how these five themes emerge as the core to Jesus' understanding of the meaning and purpose of life and the place of the Divine within life. But, underneath it all is a deep truth that stretches throughout. It may well be referred to as the implicit or ultimate theme (sutra) of Jesus. It is the understanding that we can know nothing of the substance of life, know nothing of the life spiritual or, for that matter, know nothing genuine about the Divine apart from relationship.

BELIEF IN IDEAS AS A WAY OF KNOWING THE DIVINE: THE ERROR OF CLASSIC CHRISTIANITY

As we already explored in the last chapter, the motivations of Constantine to make Christianity a unifying force in the Roman Empire set Christianity, as a religion, on a path in which faith became defined by right thought and right belief. The obsession of control and dominance that engulfed the Church for the next 1,600 years, and continues in many respects to do so now, is based upon the assumption that faithfulness and knowledge of the Divine comes through intellectual submission to a specific set of ideas about the Divine and a specific way of interpreting scriptures within that intellectual framework. The ramifications of this pattern have been huge when we look at how Christianity has developed over the years. There have been both positive and negative (mostly negative) developments in the history of the Christian faith.

One of the positive dimensions of that model is that it brought a discreet amount of certainty to the practice of faith. It allowed those who were not predisposed to mystery or a mystical approach to religion to pattern their lives on an established set of moral rules and to have a sense of one's place in relationship to the Divine. It made it possible to have some sense of certainty about the place of the Divine, and one's own place in the Universe. It also provided a set of answers to most of life's most troubling questions, including questions about suffering and the end of life.

Another positive dimension of such a model is that it ultimately led to what became known as the scientific revolution. The faith system of Western Christianity was built on the idea that faith was a quantifiable truth and that the Divine could be understood from the evidences of scripture and God's works in history. Such a faith system, built on a philosophically motivated paradigm, allowed for the development of inquiry that sought out the "fingerprints of the God" in the natural world.[50] But, in almost every other regard, this self-same faith system moved the experience of the Divine and the question of faith away from how one lives to what one believes. Such a move has had significant negative effects.

If as a child you ever heard the words "do as I say, not as I do" you recognize the hollow tone of a faith system based on thought rather than practice. History is replete with examples of "faithful"

Christians who engage in notorious behavior, but are nonetheless held up as exemplars of faith because of their right thought.

Wars, such as the Crusades, were fought on the principle that the purpose of Christianity was to force others to think as we do, and should they refuse, to eliminate them. Furthermore, right belief as an understanding of true faith led to the Inquisition, heresy trials, witch burnings, and the virtual enslavement of native peoples under the banner of "missionary" work.[51]

Currently, in the US and other Western nations, the most extreme "pro-life" activists see nothing wrong with engaging in acts of violence against those who do not agree with their understanding of the "sanctity of life." And yet, they see no conflict between their violence and the values they claim to be espousing.

Theologies which emphasize the substituting sacrifice of Jesus for the sins of all humanity and the salvation of those who have faith in Christ (i.e., right belief in him), regularly create populations of people who support policies like the death penalty and reject environmental stewardship. Why? Because the life of faith and the way one lives, except in the narrowest definitions of morality, are unrelated.

Also, such systems in today's society doggedly continue to hold onto the mythical language of the Bible as something that must be affirmed as literally true. Right thought includes belief in supernatural miracles, direct divine intervention of a supernatural nature, and an affirmation of the events portrayed in the Gospels as being literal physical events. As we have already discussed, it is such systems of thought that have led many today, including many who grew up in a faith tradition, to walk away from a religious life.

RELATIONSHIP AS A PRIMARY METAPHOR: MYSTERY AND DEEPER REALITY

From our own experiences and from the history of humanity, we can see that ideas about the Divine and the belief in them serve, at best as an opiate to our fears, and at worst as delusion. The sense of certainty they provide is tenuous at best and we often find ourselves doing one of two things: shifting our certainties with the perpetual advent of new information,[52] or living in denial and praying that our certainties will be justified.

This pattern was just as common in the first century as it is today. Jesus challenged this pattern with another way of practicing faith (i.e., spirituality). It is exemplified in each of his themes and forms the foundational principle for his understanding of the Divine and his understanding of humanity. Rather than accepting one idea or another as true and then working to convince or coerce the world to adopt it, Jesus instead invites us to encounter the Divine in relationship.

However, to say that he holds relationship as the central metaphor is to do more than to say he wants us to have relationships. It goes far beyond that and draws us into a way of thinking about life that, frankly, is alien to most of us who grew up in a Western first-world culture. To say that the primary metaphor of life and meaning is relationship is to reject any and all forms of objectification. It is to abandon the notion that there is any reality that we can know that is separate from ourselves. It is to embrace a fundamental truth, namely that everything we experience includes us and therefore is as much about us as it is about what we are experiencing. It is to recognize that we are inextricably connected to everyone and everything, and we are incapable of separating ourselves from that reality. It is to accept that our perceptions are as much a part of reality as a measurable "truth," and that even when we go about the task of replicating and measuring an experience, for it to have any meaning it is still dependent upon what we bring to it. In other words there is nothing and no one with whom we do not have a relationship. If we open ourselves up to a relational way of understanding ourselves and the world in which we live, a universe of mystery unfolds before us.

If we stop to think about it, the idea that everything is about relationship is not such a radical idea. From the moment we are conceived we are bound by relationship. Whether it is as a fetus to the woman who is carrying us, our parents in our growth and development, the teachers we have, the neighborhood in which we grow up, our nationality, our regional culture, the foods we eat, or the air we breath, all of them are dependent upon the deep, often hidden, connections that exist between us and all that is around us.

The theologian and philosopher Martin Buber wrote an important short book called *I and Thou* in which he exposes the deep truth and mystery of such a way of understanding reality. In it he labels all relationships that objectify the world and people around us as an "I-It" relationship. But those relationships that recognize and honor the deep mystery of the other, and that recognize the steady give and take between what we perceive and the perceiver are termed as "I-Thou" relationships.

When we stop thinking of the world around us as a bunch of its, as things that can be completely described by definitions of content and context (i.e., quantified and qualified), what we discover is that life is filled with a lot more mystery than we ever recognized.

As an example of this, let's do a little experiment. Take a moment and think of someone who you know quite well and imagine them in your mind. Picture everything you know about them: the color of their hair; the shape of their face, hands, and body; the way they smell; and, what they might wear. Picture their gestures, mannerisms, way of speaking, and the way they respond and react to others. What do they love? What do they hate? What is their favorite color? Favorite book? Favorite movie? What else is that makes them unique? If this is someone you particularly like what is it that makes him or her so special? If it someone you don't like what is it that irritates you? Get as complete a picture of them in your mind as you possibly can. Got it? Okay. Even if you have known this person your whole life what you have just imagined constitutes, at best one-half of the reality that makes up this person.

In the realm of psychology there is a well-established model that describes this reality of self-knowledge and its relationship to what others know about you. It's called the Johari Window.[53]

Known Self	Hidden Self
Things we know about ourselves and others know about us	Things we know about ourselves and others do not know
Blind Self	**Unknown Self**
Things others know about us that we do not know	Things neither we nor others know about us

What this model suggests is that at any given time there are things we know about ourselves that we choose not to share with the world around us. We all know about these things. They constitute the thoughts we censor from others (e.g., our fantasies, our fears, etc.). There are also those things we know about ourselves that we share with others that constitute the social self we put out to the world. These are the things we know about ourselves that others know as well. But there are things, which are a part of social environment, which convey deep truth about us that others know that we do not know ourselves. Often these things go unmentioned because they are so obvious to others that they assume we know them about ourselves. On the occasions that someone shares such an insight it can be a monumental occasion for learning because it opens up a dimension of self-knowledge of which we have not even been aware. Finally, in this chart there are those things, which we do not know about ourselves and no one else knows either. This is the place of deep mystery.

While Buber did not once reference this psychological model it opens up the radical truth to which he points. I-Thou relationships call us to recognize the reality that we do not know everything there is to know about ourselves, nor do we know everything there is to know about others. But through a process of relationship the panes of this window can open to us, preparing us to step into a place of deep mystery and be open to the fourth pane of the window.

Buber's term for the fourth pane is the "Eternal Thou." It is the place where we set aside any pretext of knowledge and become open to what we don't know. It is a place of respect, mutuality, trust, vulnerability, and commitment. It is, in short, yet another invitation into chesed. But now any sentimentality is gone. This is no romantic notion of love, but one that is grounded in a willingness to set aside all preconceptions and all projections. When we step into such a place of relational respect we encounter the "Eternal Thou," we encounter the Divine.

Of course, such an encounter comes in the context of lived experience. It is not some abstract idea to be grasped and then "monkey-wrenched" into one's life. No, it is only out of the context of our lives that we can find the Divine. This was Jesus' point. Religious systems, when they become extractions of life, are nothing more than a distraction from or a substitute for any kind of real encounter with the Divine. The practice of religion is meant to be a means of having a shared experience of the Divine that is intentional and explicit, not a means of establishing a method of controlling thought about the Divine, or worse a means of predetermining truth.

Jesus invites us in each of these themes, individually and in all of them collectively, to a way of engaging life that is radically different from the religious traditions with which we have been shaped in the West. It is an invitation to come back to the truth of our lived experience. It is an invitation to that experience from a new perspective. It is an invitation to embrace the Divine in the midst of life, in the midst of living, in the relationships we have, and in the world in which we live.

Jesus continues to call to us across the millennia to the truth of loving and living. He calls us to know the Divine in a way that will transform humanity. He calls us to be agents of transformation and to be transformed ourselves by the radical idea of love: love of self and other, love of all that was, that is, and that will be. May we know and be known by that love always.

BIBLIOGRAPHY

Anselm of Canterbury, *Cur Deus Homo*. Fort Worth: RDMc Publishing, 2005.

Aquinas, Thomas. *Summa Theologica*. Notre Dame, IN: Christian Classics, 1981.

Borg, Marcus. *Speaking Christian: Why Christian Words Have Lost Their Meaning and Power - And How They Can Be Restored*. San Francisco: Harper One, 2011.

Brown, Raymond. *Anchor Bible Commentary: The Gospel of John*. New Haven: Yale University Press, 1995.

Buber, Martin. *I and Thou*. New York: Charles Scribner's Sons, 1970.

Crossan, John Dominic. *The Birth of Christianity: Discovering What Happened in the Years Immediately After the Execution of Jesus*. San Francisco: Harper One, 1998.

Crossan, John Dominic. *The Greatest Prayer: Rediscovering the Revolutionary Message of the Lord's Prayer*. San Francisco: Harper One, 2011.

Crossan, J.D. and M. Borg. *The Last Week - What the Gospels Really Teach About Jesus's Final Days in Jerusalem*. New York: Harper Collins, 2006.

Ehrman, Bart D. *Misquoting Jesus: The Story Behind Who Changed the Bible and Why*. San Francisco: Harper One, 2007.

Gomes, Peter J. *The Scandalous Gospel of Jesus: What's So Good About the Good News*. New York: Harper Collins, 2007.

Grenz, Stanley J. *The Social God and the Relational Self: A Trinitarian Theology of the Imago Dei*. Louisville, Kentucky: Westminster John Knox Press, 2001.

BIBLIOGRAPHY

Hannam, James. *The Genesis of Science: How the Christian Middle Ages Launched the Scientific Revolution*. Washington, DC: Regnery Publishing, 2011.

Josephus. *Josephus: The Jewish War Books III-IV (Loeb Classical Library No. 487)*. Cambridge, MA: Harvard University Press, 1979.

Lipton, Bruce. *The Biology of Belief: Unleashing the Power of Consciousness, Matter, & Miracles*. Carlsbad, CA: Hay House, 2008.

Muffs, Yochanan. *The Personhood of God: Biblical Theology, Human Faith And the Divine Image*. Woodstock, Vermont: Jewish Lights Publishing, 2005.

Otto, Rudolph. *The Idea of the Holy*. Oxford, England: Oxford University Press, 1958.

Pilch, John J. *The Cultural World of Jesus, Sunday by Sunday Cycles A, B, and C*. Collegeville, MN: Liturgical Press, 1997.

Ricoeur, Paul. *Symbolism of Evil*. New York: Harper & Row, 1969.

Segal, Alan. *Life After Death: A History of the Afterlife in Western Tradition*. New York: Doubleday, 2004.

Spong, John Shelby. *Jesus for the Non-Religious*. San Francisco: Harper One, 2007.

NOTES

1   The search for meaning and/or truth in language has two
    rational disciplines of inquiry within philosophical thought.
    Hermeneutics is the rational pursuit of meaning in language,
    while epistemology is the equally rational pursuit of truth and
    knowledge in general.

2   Of greatest influence were the works of John J. Pilch, John P.
    Meier, Raymond Brown, John Dominic Crossan, and Marcus
    Borg.

3   This point is not to equate Judaism with Hinduism, Buddhism,
    Taoism, or Confucianism, but to convey that especially in the
    teaching and mystical traditions (e.g., *midrash*) of Judaism (e.g.,
    Kabbalah) there are overtly Eastern patterns to this Abrahamic
    faith.

4   An academic term to convey the time period commonly marked
    with the letters "AD" after the year (i.e., 2012 AD). "AD" is
    shorthand for "Anno Domini" meaning "in the year of our Lord."
    This dating system was developed in 525 by Dionysius Exiguus,
    who based his dating system upon the supposed birth year of
    Jesus of Nazareth. Although now recognized to be inaccurate
    because of the vagaries of the Julian calendar and a variety
    computing errors, it has become a standard dating system for
    the Western world. Because of its overly religious overtones AD
    has been substituted within academic circles with CE
    (representing "Common Era").

5   Zeno, Archimedes, and Pythagoras are but a few of the well-
    known names associated with this phase of what we have come
    to call Greek philosophy. BCE ~ "Before the Common Era" see
    note 4 for more.

6   There are 46 parables if one accepts Jesus' reference to himself
    as the "good shepherd" and the "sheep gate" in the Gospel of
    John as a parable. If not then there are only 44 parables and they
    are all contained in Matthew, Mark, and Luke.

NOTES

7   *Merriam-Webster Online* (http://www.merriam-webster.com/dictionary/religion)

8   As an example one only need to look at any number of popular songs from the last half-century to see the isolating nature of self-consciousness (e.g., "I Am A Rock" by Simon and Garfunkel, or "Behind Blue Eyes" by The Who).

9   Alan Segal, *Life After Death: A History of the Afterlife in Western Tradition* (New York: Doubleday, 2004), 355.

10 A similar version of this story occurs in Luke 18:18-23

11 Bruce Lipton, *The Biology of Belief* (Carlsbad, CA: Hay House, 2008), Chapter 5.

12 This effect was first recognized in classical Greek times. Aristotle noted that drama could create powerful emotions that would have a refreshing and purifying impact on the spectators. He called this effect "catharsis." The word itself is a Greek word meaning "purgation" or "cleansing."

13 While the word used in the Gospel of John is the Greek word "ora" for "hour," the use of hour by Jesus in this context points to the notion of the in-breaking reality of the Divine into his life and the life of his followers and points to a notion of kairos.

14 S.G.F. Brandon, "The Origin of Death in Some Ancient Near Eastern Religions," *Religious Studies, Vol. 1, No. 2* (Apr. 1966) (Cambridge: Cambridge University Press), 217.

15 "So God created humankind in his image, in the image of God he created them; male and female he created them." (Genesis 1:27)

16 There are any number of books that can be read on this topic. Of interest from a Jewish perspective might be *The Personhood of God: Biblical Theology, Human Faith And the Divine Image* by Yochanan Muffs (Woodstock, Vermont: Jewish Lights Publishing, 2005). A current Christian perspective might be gained by reading *The Social God and the Relational Self: A Trinitarian Theology of the Imago Dei* by Stanley J. Grenz (Louisville, Kentucky: Westminster John Knox Press, 2001).

17 According to a 2004 poll by Gallup, 83% of Americans believed in an afterlife. (http://www.gallup.com/poll/11770/eternal-destinations-americans-believe-heaven-hell.aspx)

18 There were at least five messianic figures in or around the first century C.E. The best known, Simon bar Kochba, is recorded by the historian Josephus in his book *The Jewish War*. Bar Kochba led an extended Jewish revolt resulting in three years of Jewish independence from the Roman Empire in the year 132 CE. He was ultimately defeated and killed by the Romans in 135 CE. There were a number of both Gentile and Jewish miracle workers in the first century. Best known is Hanina ben Dosa, who is reported to have been a rainmaker (Ta'anit, 24b).

19 In less than 150 years between the turn of the millennium and 150 CE there were three major Jewish revolts in the Holy Land. In the midst of these revolts the Temple in Jerusalem was destroyed by the Romans in the year 70 CE.

20 A similar account occurs in Luke 22.

21 In rabbinical Judaism love of God and love of neighbor are linked through the works of Philo and Josephus in works titled the "Letter of Aristeas" and the "Testaments of the Twelve Patriarchs." (Ulrich Luz, *Hermeneia: Matthew 21-28* (2005: Augsburg Fortress), 84.).

22 As was noted earlier, the count of the total number of parables is a source of discrepancy. There are counts as low as 40 and as high as 46. This variation is dependent on how one determines whether a saying of Jesus is a metaphor, an analogy, or a parable. There are minimally 40 upon which most sources agree and possibly another five or six depending on the degree to which one is willing to count them as parable.

23 "Guideline on Teaching Storytelling - A Position Statement from the Committee on Storytelling, 1992," http://www.ncte.org/positions/statements/teachingstorytelling.

24 Commentary on Deuteronomy 6:4-9, *Interpreters Bible*

Commentary, Vol. 2 (Nashville: Abingdon Press, 1953), 373-374.

25 *The Journal for the Society of Textual Reasoning*, Volume 4, Number 1, November, 2005; Kenneth Reinhard, "The Ethics of the Neighbor: Universalism, Particularism, Exceptionalism," University of California, Los Angeles.

26 Elster, J., "Social Norms and Economic Theory," in *Journal of Economic Perspectives, Volume 3, Number 4*, 1989.

27 Most of the Ten Commandments found in Exodus 20 are placed in the negative. But even the injunction to "honor your father and mother," while positive in its language, lays down an implied threat and comes in response to numerous examples in earlier biblical texts where such behavior was in short supply.

28 It is interesting to note that laws regarding theft, violence, and sexuality are the most common laws in most societies. When one stops to think about it, these laws deal with issues of stability, sustainability, generativity, and mortality.

29 A good example of such a time in American history was the debate over the morality of the war in Vietnam in the 1960s and '70s. Those who supported the war and those who protested it appealed to differing authorities to support their actions. Both spoke passionately from their position and felt justified in it because of the authorities to which they appealed. Needless to say each denied the legitimacy of the other's authority.

30 Geoffrey Sayre-McCord, "The Many Moral Realisms" in *Essays on Moral Realism*, ed. Sayre-McCord (Ithaca: Cornell University Press, 1988).

31 Thomas Aquinas argues that the rational nature of human beings is what defines moral law: "The rule and measure of human acts is the reason, which is the first principle of human acts." (Aquinas, ST I-II, Q.90, A.I).

32 The Lord passed before him, and proclaimed, "The Lord, the Lord, a God merciful and gracious, slow to anger, and abounding in steadfast love and faithfulness, keeping steadfast love for the thousandth generation, forgiving iniquity and transgression and

sin, yet by no means clearing the guilty, but visiting the iniquity of the parents upon the children and the children's children, to the third and the fourth generation." (Exodus 34:6-7)

33 His disciples asked him, "Rabbi, who sinned, this man or his parents, that he was born blind?" (John 9:2)

34 A clear example of this occurs in regard to the woman who is to be stoned for adultery (John 8:1-11). After Jesus has guilted the crowd into leaving and told the woman that he does not condemn her either, he concludes the dialogue with the admonition, "Go and sin no more." Her sin, adultery, is still seen as sin because of the inherent issues of objectification involved in such behavior. The use of other people as sexual objects, or the justification of such behavior by objectifying one's spouse is a violation of Jesus' notion of the love that we are called to express and accept from one another. His response to her represents a radically different way of engaging her than the domination system would have.

35 The 39 forbidden activities (in Hebrew, *malachot*) are: Sowing, Plowing, Reaping, Binding Sheaves, Threshing, Winnowing, Selecting, Grinding, Sifting, Kneading, Baking, Shearing, Bleaching, Hackling, Dyeing, Spinning, Stretching the threads, the making of two meshes, Weaving two threads, Dividing two threads, Tying a knot, Untying a knot, Sewing two stitches, Tearing in order to sew two stitches, Capturing (an animal), Slaughtering, Flaying, Salting, Curing hide, Scraping, Cutting, Writing two letters, Erasing in order to write two letters, Building, Demolishing, Extinguishing fire, Kindling fire, Striking with a hammer (i.e. giving something its final touch), Carrying (in a public domain, or from a private domain to a public domain, and vice versa).

36 This is not to imply that the spiritual disciplines of Judaism around Sabbath observance are in any way invalid or unimportant. It is clear that Jesus himself took Sabbath seriously. The subsequent developments of rabbinical Judaism and the rigor with which interpretation of Torah became

collected in the Talmud and other writings is a benefit to all humanity. Rather the point in this paragraph is to make clear the ways in which rule making, as a means of reducing anxiety, become masked with other values that do not, in fact, motivate the rules. The model of Sabbath imposition at the time of Jesus is such an example.

37 Healing the withered hand of man (Matthew 12:9-21, Mark 3:1-6, Luke 6:6-11); Jesus heals a paralytic at the Pool of Bethesda (John 5:9-18); Jesus equates healing someone to circumcision on the Sabbath (John 7:21-23); Jesus healing a man born blind from birth (John 9); Jesus heals a woman bent over from the pain of a spirit (Luke 13:10-17); Jesus heals a man with dropsy (Luke 14:1-6); and, Jesus and his disciples accused of reaping on the Sabbath (Mark 2:23-28).

38 This understanding is not only supported by Jesus' own teaching but by subsequent rabbinical teaching found in the Talmud and other sources. See the Talmud (B. Yoma 84b) for a number of examples in which the violation of the Sabbath to save a human life is seen as a moral act.

39 This is to distinguish Jesus' understanding of the good news from that of his followers, who later came to understand the "good news" to be the proclamation of Jesus' teaching, life, death, and resurrection. It is from this later idea of "good news" that the word gospel is derived (old English "gōd spell"="good news").

40 Yahweh is a hypothesized pronunciation of the name of the Divine in the Hebrew scriptures. The absence of vowels in the writing of the name has resulted in a number of different approaches to dealing with the Divine name (i.e., Jehovah, the Lord, etc.).

41 Rudolf Otto, *The Idea of the Holy* (Oxford: Oxford University Press, 1958).

42 Arthur E. Cundall, "Sacral Kingship—The Old Testament Background," *Vox Evangelica 6* (1969): 31-41.

43 Even ancient democracies often resorted to domination systems. Ancient Greece and the Roman Republic, more often than not, had limited democracies in which the ability to rule was not available to all.

44 Some translations choose to translate the Greek text verb *engizdo* as "has come near," while others "is at hand." A general understanding of the verb is that its general meaning is "has drawn near." However, the verb connotes immediacy and imminence and so we will use the term "is at hand" as the preferred understanding of the term.

45 "Eschatology", *Oxford Dictionary of the Christian Church, 3rd Edition*, F.L. Cross & E.A. Livingstone, eds. (Oxford: Oxford University Press, 2005).

46 For more on how Crossan uses this idea look at his book *The Birth of Christianity: Discovering What Happened in the Years Immediately After the Execution of Jesus* (San Francisco: Harper One, 1998).

47 "Will you seek and serve Christ in all persons and love your neighbor as yourself?" is a question asked of those to be baptized in the Episcopal Church as a part of what is termed the "Baptismal Covenant." See *Book of Common Prayer of the Episcopal Church* (New York: Church Publishing, 1979).

48 For example, a popular understanding of Jesus in the early fourth century that was later declared a heresy was that Jesus as a human being was, in fact, an illusion and that his death on the cross never actually happened. While there was the image of a death, he actually did not suffer because his body was not real. This was because if Jesus were divine it would be impossible for him to be material and divine at the same time. This theological understanding of Jesus was termed Docetism.

49 To be clear, there was ample debate in the first three centuries of Christianity. Such debates included: the nature of God, Jesus, the Spirit; the place of Judaism within Christian tradition; what constitutes moral or immoral behavior; and the place and role of

different peoples in the church. But, churches existed side by side without fear of destruction by the other.

50 For more information on how the Christian Middle Ages launched the scientific revolution see James Hannam's *The Genesis of Science* (Washington, DC: Regnery Publishing, 2011).

51 The beatification of Junipero Serra, founder of the Franciscan missions of California, in 1988 was strongly objected to by Native American groups who pointed out that the missions seriously mistreated their people. (James A. Sandos, "Junipero Serra, Cannonization, and the California Indian Controversy" in *Journal of Religious History vol. 15 no. 3*, June 1989).

52 This is sometimes referred to as the belief in the "God of the gaps." For more see the writings of Henry Drummond, Dietrich Bonhoeffer, and Charles Alfred Coulson.

53 Luft, J., Ingham, H. (1950). "The Johari window, a graphic model of interpersonal awareness." Proceedings of the western training laboratory in group development (Los Angeles: UCLA).